Financial Inclusion, Remittance Inflows, and Poverty Reduction in Developing Countries:

Evidence from Empirical Analyses

Financial Inclusion, Remittance Inflows, and Poverty Reduction in Developing Countries:
Evidence from Empirical Analyses

Takeshi Inoue • Shigeyuki Hamori

Kobe University, Japan

World Scientific

EW JERSEY • LONDON • SINGAPORE • BEIJING • SHANGHAI • HONG KONG • TAIPEI • CHENNAI • TOKYO

Published by

World Scientific Publishing Co. Pte. Ltd.

5 Toh Tuck Link, Singapore 596224

USA office: 27 Warren Street, Suite 401-402, Hackensack, NJ 07601

UK office: 57 Shelton Street, Covent Garden, London WC2H 9HE

Library of Congress Control Number: 2018060914

British Library Cataloguing-in-Publication Data
A catalogue record for this book is available from the British Library.

ISBN 978-981-3278-92-9

For any available supplementary material, please visit
https://www.worldscientific.com/worldscibooks/10.1142/11231#t=suppl

Desk Editor: Lum Pui Yee

Typeset by Stallion Press
Email: enquiries@stallionpress.com

Printed in Singapore

About the Authors

Takeshi INOUE is an Associate Professor at the Graduate School of International Cooperation Studies, Kobe University, Japan. He received his Ph.D. in Economics from Kobe University. His research interests include financial inclusion, international remittances, and Indian economy. He is the co-author of India Economy: Empirical Analysis on Monetary and Financial Issues in India (World Scientific, 2014) and Financial Linkages, Remittances, and Resource Dependence in East Asia (World Scientific, 2015).

Shigeyuki HAMORI is a Professor of Economics, Graduate School of Economics, Kobe University, Japan. He holds a Ph.D. in Economics from Duke University, the United States. His main research interests are applied time series analysis, empirical finance, data science, and international finance. He has published about 200 articles in international peer-reviewed journals. He serves on the editorial boards of several academic journals.

List of Abbreviations

AFI	Alliance for Financial Inclusion
CPI	consumer price index
DOLS	dynamic ordinary least squares
EAP	East Asia and the Pacific
FAS	Financial Access Survey
FDI	foreign direct investment
FMOLS	fully modified ordinary least squares
GMM	generalized method of moments
G20	Group of 20
IMF	International Monetary Fund
LAC	Latin America and the Caribbean
MENA	Middle East and North Africa
MFIs	microfinance institutions
MIX	Microfinance Information Exchange
ODA	official development assistance
OLS	ordinary least squares
SMEs	small and medium enterprises
2SLS	two-stage least squares
3SLS	three-stage least squares

Contents

Chapter 3. Remittance Inflows and Economic Growth: Clarifying Conflicting Results in the Literature   37

Chapter 4. Remittance Inflows and Poverty Reduction: How Economic Development Affects Remittances' Effect on Poverty Reduction   85

List of Figures

List of Tables

Introduction

There is ample evidence to prove a strong causal relationship between the depth of the financial system, on the one hand, and investment, growth, and total factor productivity on the other (Claessens, 2006). Much of this evidence specifically examines the importance of financial development, typically designated as "financial deepening," which is perceived as an increase in the proportion of the financial sector in the real economy. However, in many developing countries, the financial system does not primarily cater to the needs of all types of customers and is skewed toward those who are already better off (*ibid.*, 2006). Accordingly, in addition to financial deepening, "financial inclusion" has also received a great deal of attention of late.

Financial inclusion is a multi-dimensional concept and is generally regarded as the process of ensuring access to and usage of basic formal financial services provided by formal and semi-formal financial intermediaries to everyone at an affordable price. Basic formal financial services include credit, savings, insurance, payments, and remittance facilities. People in developing countries, particularly those in low-income countries, are sometimes forced to rely on informal and expensive sources of finance when they are unable to use basic financial services, or lack access to them; this reliance on inadequate facilities endangers their already precarious financial circumstances. Therefore, financial inclusion expands the possibilities for using reasonably priced basic financial services and contributes to economic growth and poverty reduction in developing countries.

In recent years, remittances from overseas workers have also received attention as a source of finance to promote economic growth and reduce poverty in developing countries. Beginning in the early 2000s, the amount of international remittances from overseas workers to their families in developing countries have expanded dramatically, as of 2012 becoming equivalent to half the total value of foreign direct investment (FDI) and four times the value of official development assistance (ODA) received by developing countries. Additional income in the form of remittances enables recipient families to increase and smooth their expenditure. They can raise their standard of living by improving sanitation facilities and increasing investment in education (International Monetary Fund, 2005). In addition, because remittances are private unrequited income transfers between individuals, they are more effective than other primary sources of external funds, such as FDI and ODA, for increasing incomes and reducing poverty in developing countries.

As explained above, financial inclusion and remittance inflows both indicate the potential of finance to resolve issues of growth and poverty in developing countries, which has been demonstrated by many empirical analyses using macro datasets. Prior research has confirmed that remittance inflows promote financial deepening and financial inclusion and contribute to poverty alleviation directly and indirectly through financial deepening. While studies on remittances have supported their positive effects on poverty reduction, they have not led to agreement on their effectiveness in ensuring economic growth in recipient countries. Based on a wide-ranging review of prior research and empirical analyses from a new perspective, this book aims to systematically clarify the relations between financial inclusion, remittance inflows, economic growth, and poverty reduction in developing countries, and seeks to reveal a new role for development finance.

Financial deepening, an increase in the scale of the financial sector in the real economy, is usually measured by the value of bank credit, bank deposits, or monetary aggregates relative to a country's GDP. On the other hand, different indicators measure financial inclusion. For example, Beck *et al.* (2007) used data on the number of bank branches and automated teller machines per capita and per square kilometer to measure the access dimension of financial inclusion, and used data on the number of loan accounts and deposit accounts per capita and the average loan and deposit size relative to GDP per capita to measure the usage dimension of financial inclusion.

Similarly, the Alliance for Financial Inclusion (AFI) (2013) defined financial inclusion as the process of ensuring access to and usage of banking services. The AFI measured the access dimension by the number of bank facilities per 10,000 adults, the percentage of administrative units with at least one bank facility, and the percentage of total population living in administrative units with at least one bank facility. In addition, the AFI measured the usage dimension by the percentage of adults with at least one type of bank account or the number of accounts per 10,000 adults.

Following Beck *et al.* (2007) and the AFI (2013), we measure the degree of financial inclusion in terms of access to and/or usage of basic financial services provided by commercial banks or microfinance institutions (MFIs). More specifically, in Chapters 1 and 5, we use the number of bank branches as the indicator of financial inclusion, whereas in Chapters 2 and 6, we use the number of MFIs and/or the number of active borrowers from MFIs as the indicator of financial inclusion. Furthermore, we measure the degree of financial deepening by the ratio of money supply to GDP and the ratio of credit to GDP in Chapter 1, MFIs' gross loan portfolio per capita in Chapter 2, and the ratio of bank deposits to GDP and the ratio of bank loans to GDP in Chapter 5. In these chapters, we compare the empirical results of financial inclusion and financial deepening.

Figure 0.1 depicts the relations among the chapters in this book. A summary of each chapter is the following.

Chapters 1 and 2 analyze the effects of financial inclusion on economic growth and poverty reduction in developing countries. Financial inclusion in developing countries, which promotes access to and use of basic financial services provided by formal and semi-formal financial intermediaries at a reasonable price, is expected to remedy credit unavailability among poor people who have not yet used the services of financial institutions. This would increase

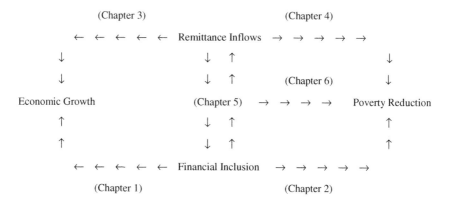

Figure 0.1   Relations among the Chapters

their income by stimulating economic activity and alleviate poverty. In Chapter 1, we empirically analyze whether improved access to banking services has contributed to economic growth and find that financial inclusion has a statistically significant and robust effect of increasing economic growth. In Chapter 2, we measure the degree of financial inclusion using indicators related to MFIs and examine the effect of greater financial inclusion on poverty. The results show that financial inclusion has a statistically significant and robust effect of decreasing the poverty ratio.

Chapters 3 and 4 analyze the effects of remittance inflows on economic growth and poverty reduction. Prior research addressing the effect of remittances on economic growth has remained inconclusive. Chapter 3 offers a new perspective on earlier studies by including the square of remittances as a regressor to elucidate the nonlinear effect of remittances on economic growth. Our empirical results suggest that the relationship between remittances and growth has an inverted U-shape and that the effect of remittances on economic growth might change from positive to negative over time. Unlike the effect of remittances on economic growth, earlier studies have shown the direct effect and the indirect effect through income distribution of remittances on poverty reduction in developing countries. Chapter 4 differs from the reviewed literature in that it examines whether the effect of remittances on poverty changes as an economy develops.

Our results show that the effect of remittances on reducing poverty is influenced by the income level of the recipient country: the higher the recipient country's income level per capita, the weaker this effect becomes.

Chapter 5 analyzes the relation between financial inclusion and remittance inflows. Because of the growing recognition of the usefulness of finance in economic growth and poverty reduction, more studies are being undertaken to ascertain the factors that encourage financial development. While previous studies have described that an increase in remittances results in greater financial deepening, Chapter 5 focuses on the access to formal financial services and empirically analyzes whether and how remittance inflows affect financial inclusion. The results show that greater demand for financial services by those receiving remittances from overseas family members promotes financial inclusion in developing countries.

Finally, Chapter 6 analyzes the relations among financial inclusion, remittance inflows, and their influences on poverty reduction in developing countries. Prior literature has demonstrated that financial inclusion and remittance inflows are effective in reducing poverty, with their effects of raising living standards and remedying the dearth of capital among poor people. However, observing that the main beneficiaries of financial inclusion — poor people in developing countries — begin to use remittance services while working overseas, it seems that a relation exists between progress in financial inclusion and international remittances that help to reduce poverty. Chapter 6 examines the relation between the two variables through a model estimating the intersection of financial inclusion and remittance inflows, with the finding that synergies arising from expanded access to MFIs and greater remittance inflows are useful to reduce poverty in developing countries.

This book is the result of our collaborative research. We dedicate this book to our family members, who have been steadfast in their support of our research activities, without which it would not have been possible for us to prepare and publish this book. This book was supported by JSPS KAKENHI Grant Numbers JP17K03687 and JP17K18564. Finally, we would like to show our appreciation to

Ms. Lum Pui Yee at World Scientific Publishing for her outstanding assistance in editing and publishing this book.

References

Alliance for Financial Inclusion (AFI), 2013. *Measuring Financial Inclusion: Core Set of Financial Inclusion Indicators*. AFI, Bangkok.

Beck, T., Demirgüç-Kunt, A., Martínez Pería, M. S., 2007. Reaching out: Access to and use of banking services across countries. *Journal of Financial Economics* 85, 234–266.

Claessens, S., 2006. Access to financial services: A review of the issues and public policy objectives. *The World Bank Research Observer* 21, 207–240.

International Monetary Fund (IMF), 2005. *World Economic Outlook April 2005: Globalization and External Imbalances*. IMF, Washington D.C.

Chapter 1

Financial Inclusion and Economic Growth: Is Banking Breadth Important for Economic Growth?

1.1 Introduction

Country-level and regional-level research efforts have often demonstrated that financial development is an integral factor in a country's economic growth (King and Levine, 1993; Demirgüç-Kunt and Maksimovic, 1996; Levine and Zervos, 1998; Graff, 2003) and that a positive bidirectional relationship exists between financial development and economic growth (Demetriades and Hussein, 1996; Luintel and Khan, 1999; Kirkpatrick, 2000; Apergis et al., 2007). In these various studies, the provision of financial intermediation is typically designated as "financial deepening." This is defined as the increased scale of the financial sector in the real economy, such as bank credit, bank deposits, and/or monetary aggregates all normalized by a country's GDP.

In contrast to the current body of knowledge, we empirically examine the role of finance in the economic growth of developing countries from the perspective of the so-called "financial inclusion." Financial inclusion in general and financial access in particular are expected to promote the accessibility and convenience of financial services provided by financial intermediaries by establishing an extensive national network rather than by expanding scale. According to this concept, financial inclusion contributes to economic growth by reducing funding constraints and promoting the economic activities of individuals and companies that had been previously unable to use financial services. Although several types of intermediaries can be envisioned as major players in improved financial inclusion, the focus here is on commercial banks as traditional providers of financial services in developing countries.

Specifically, we construct proxy measures of the accessibility of financial services among users based on the number of commercial bank branches in terms of a demographic or geographic measure. We use panel data from 168 countries between 2004 and 2014 to estimate the effect of financial inclusion on economic growth. In addition, we consider the education level and macroeconomic variables, such as the investment ratio and economic openness, which have been accepted in related studies as important factors contributing to economic growth. Furthermore, instead of using measures of financial inclusion, we use traditional measures of financial deepening, such as the ratio of money supply to GDP and the ratio of credit to GDP, to confirm the effect of financial deepening on economic growth.[1]

This chapter is organized as follows. Section 1.2 explains the relevant literature. Section 1.3 presents our model and Section 1.4 provides the definitions, sources, and properties of the data. Section 1.5 explains the empirical technique. Section 1.6 presents the empirical results. Section 1.7 summarizes the major findings.

1.2   Literature Review

In recent years, such phrases as "financial inclusion" and "finance for all" have been embraced as new policy objectives by international

---

[1]Inoue and Hamori (2016) analyze the relationship between financial access and economic growth using panel data from 37 sub-Saharan African countries between 2004 and 2012. This chapter retains this analytical framework using panel data from 168 countries between 2004 and 2014. Furthermore, whereas Inoue and Hamori (2016) use two measures of financial deepening, that is, outstanding deposits with commercial banks as a percentage of GDP and outstanding loans from commercial banks as a percentage of GDP, this chapter uses the more traditional measures of financial deepening, namely, money and quasi-money (M2) as a percentage of GDP and domestic credit to the private sector by banks as a percentage of GDP.

organizations including the World Bank, Asian Development Bank, and Group of 20 (G20), and by certain developing countries (e.g., Brazil, India, and Indonesia). The aim of financial inclusion is to allow everyone to receive the benefits of economic growth by creating an environment in which all potential users can access financial services. Beneficiaries include "unbanked" individuals who have not been offered financial services, such as credit, savings, and money wiring, and "underbanked" individuals who have not used financial services even though they have access to them.

As increasing attention has been paid to the subject of improving access and convenience of financial services in recent years, we have begun to observe the development of databases of related indicators. Some well-known databases include the Financial Access Survey (FAS) by the International Monetary Fund (IMF) and the Global Financial Inclusion Index (Global Findex) and Enterprise Surveys by the World Bank.[2] Analyses using these databases are currently underway to verify such increased access and convenience by country or region. For example, Demirgüç-Kunt and Klapper (2012a) use the World Bank's 2012 Global Findex database to examine how adults in 148 countries save and borrow money, make payments, and manage risks during the year 2011. The authors report that approximately half the adult population worldwide remains unbanked and that at least 35% of adults face barriers to using bank accounts. Although these barriers vary based on regional and individual characteristics, high costs, physical distance, and lack of appropriate procedural documents are noted as the most common barriers.

Demirgüç-Kunt and Klapper (2012b) use the 2012 Global Findex database and Enterprise Surveys to examine the access of individuals and small and medium enterprises (SMEs) to banking in African countries. The authors find that less than a quarter of adults in

---

[2]In addition, the G20 Basic Set of Financial Inclusion Indicators and Core Set of Financial Inclusion Indicators have been developed to capture the state of financial inclusion in a country by the Global Partnership for Financial Inclusion and the Alliance for Financial Inclusion's Financial Inclusion Data Working Group, respectively. These indicators are based on existing data sources, such as the FAS, Global Findex, and Enterprise Surveys.

Africa have an account with a formal financial institution and that many adults in Africa use informal methods to save and borrow. In addition, the authors find that most SMEs in Africa are unbanked and that access to finance is a major obstacle.

Allen *et al.* (2014) employ five measures of financial inclusion taken from the Global Findex database, as well as two measures of financial deepening and investigate the levels of financial inclusion and deepening in Africa. Using cross-country data of average values from 2007 to 2011, the authors find that the population density is more strongly linked to both financial inclusion and deepening in Africa than in other developing countries. Therefore, the authors conclude that "technological advances, such as mobile banking, have provided a promising way to facilitate African financial inclusion and deepening outside major cities" (Allen *et al.*, 2014, p. 16).

Mialou *et al.* (2017) construct a composite indicator of financial inclusion for 30 countries from 2009 to 2012 using the IMF's FAS database. The outreach dimension is measured by the number of automatic teller machines and branches per $1,000\,\mathrm{km}^2$; the usage dimension is measured by the number of borrowers and depositors of financial intermediaries per 1,000 adults. Factor analysis is applied to identify financial inclusion dimensions and to assign weights. Then, the authors derive the composite indicator from a nonlinear aggregation of intermediate dimensional indicators, finding that the top three countries in the composite indicator for 2011 and 2012 are Asia-Pacific nations and that eight of the bottom 10 countries are African nations.

As such, these studies have specifically elucidated regional characteristics, determinants, or barriers to financial accessibility rather than exploring the effect of financial inclusion on economic growth. Consequently, by examining this latter point, this study contributes to the existing literature.

1.3   Model

In neoclassical growth theory, as represented by Solow (1956), economic development is considered dependent on advances in technology; however, the technology level is an exogenous variable.

Neoclassical growth theory has the following characteristics: (1) in the steady state, output per capita and capital stock per capita are considered fixed; (2) the savings rate is not influenced by the growth rate per capita over the long term, but it has a consistent effect on the rate of productivity per capita in the steady state; (3) two countries with identical rates of savings and population growth converge to an equilibrium value of output per capita. That is, the poor country develops more rapidly than the richer one. However, ultimately, both countries attain the same average productivity per capita.

In response to Solow, Romer (1986) called for a new theory of economic growth that accorded importance to the role of human capital and knowledge investment. This is known as the endogenous growth theory, in which technological development does not act exogenously but is an endogenous factor in capital stock development in the broad sense that serves as a cause of economic growth.

Rebelo (1991) explains endogenous growth theory based on his AK model. Production is expressed as follows:

$$Y = AK. \tag{1.1}$$

Here, A is a constant that represents the productivity of capital stock, and K represents a broad understanding of capital that includes human capital and social infrastructure rather than just capital in its usual and narrowly material sense. The marginal productivity of this broad understanding of capital does not decrease and is assumed fixed as (A) here.

From Equation (1.1), we understand that

$$\Delta Y = A\Delta K. \tag{1.2}$$

In Equation (1.2), ΔK is the broad understanding of capital. Assuming that this is equivalent to society's total savings $(S = sY)$, we obtain the following:

$$\Delta Y = AsY. \tag{1.3}$$

Dividing both sides by Y, the rate of economic growth becomes

$$\Delta Y/Y = As. \tag{1.4}$$

Here, the rate of growth in productivity per capita ($y = Y/L$, where L is population) can be expressed as follows:

$$\Delta y/y \cong \Delta Y/Y - \Delta L/L = As - n, \qquad (1.5)$$

where n is the rate of population growth.

In contrast to neoclassical models in which the growth rate converges upon a fixed value, in the AK model, the rate of growth increases in accordance with the size of A and s, as Equation (1.5) clearly demonstrates. Therefore, the differences in the endogenous values A and s explain the differences in each country's economic growth rates.

Endogenous growth theory has the following characteristics: (1) an increase in the savings rate results in a permanent increase in the rate of productivity growth per capita; (2) irrespective of their initial level of income, poor and rich countries grow at the same rate and continue to raise their productivity per capita. Therefore, there is no convergence in the level of per capita income. This characteristic is completely at odds with neoclassical growth theory. We express the production function represented in Equation (1.1) more generally as follows:

$$Y = A(K)K. \qquad (1.6)$$

Here, the level of technology expressed by $A(K)$ is dependent on the broad understanding of capital (K). This includes material and human capital as well as research and development. Furthermore, $A(K)$ is dependent on structural elements in the economy. In this chapter, we focus on and analyze the role of financial inclusion in $A(K)$.

1.4   Data

We conducted a panel analysis using annual data of 168 countries between 2004 and 2014. Table 1.1 provides the definition and source of each variable. Table 1.2 presents summary statistics for each variable. The logarithm of real per capita GDP (GDP) is used as the dependent variable in this quantitative analysis. The data are

Table 1.1   **Definition and Source of Each Variable**

Variable	Definition	Source
GDP	Logarithm of real per capita GDP (constant 2005 US$)	World Bank (2016)
FI1	Numbers of commercial bank branches per 1,000 km^2	IMF (2016)
FI2	Numbers of commercial bank branches per 100,000 adults	
FD1	Logarithm of money and quasi-money (M2) as a percentage of GDP	World Bank (2016)
FD2	Logarithm of domestic credit to the private sector by banks as a percentage of GDP	
INVEST	Gross capital formation as a percentage of GDP	World Bank (2016)
OPEN	Exports and imports of goods and services as a percentage of GDP	
SCL	Gross primary school enrollment ratio, both sexes (%)	

Table 1.2   **Summary Statistics**

Variable	Mean	Standard Deviation	Sample Size
GDP	8.175	1.575	1,825
FI1	25.099	62.859	1,756
FI2	18.869	19.717	1,756
FD1	3.835	0.603	1,153
FD2	3.409	0.883	1,153
INVEST	24.448	8.306	1,739
OPEN	90.761	47.254	1,777
SCL	103.654	12.976	1,406

Note: Detailed variable descriptions are presented in Table 1.1.

obtained from the World Development Indicators published by the World Bank (2016). Its average value is 8.175 and the standard deviation is 1.575.

Financial inclusion in general and financial access in particular are the most important of all the explanatory variables in this study. To measure the accessibility of financial services, we use two proxy variables: the number of commercial bank branches per $1,000\,\text{km}^2 (FI1)$ and the number of commercial bank branches per 100,000 adults $(FI2)$. The data for these variables are derived from the FAS of the IMF (2016). Because improvement of financial service accessibility engenders increased economic activities among households and companies that face funding constraints, the coefficient of FI in the model is expected to be positive (Claessens, 2006; Beck *et al.*, 2008; Ellis *et al.*, 2010).

We alternatively consider financial deepening as a traditional concept of financial development and examine its effect on economic growth (Levine, 2005; Beck, 2008, 2012). We measure the degree of financial deepening using two indicators of banking sector development: the logarithm of money and quasi-money (M2) as a percentage of GDP $(FD1)$ and the logarithm of domestic credit by banks to the private sector as a percentage of GDP $(FD2)$. Credit refers to financial resources provided to the private sector by financial corporations. The data are derived from the World Bank (2016). Because developed financial intermediaries are assumed to mobilize savings effectively and channel them to productive economic sectors, the coefficient of FD in the model is expected to be positive.

Regarding other exogenous variables, we control the investment ratio $(INVEST)$, economic openness $(OPEN)$, and school enrollment ratio (SCL). The investment ratio is the ratio of gross capital formation to GDP. The data are obtained from the World Bank (2016). As Levine and Renelt (1992) and De Long and Summers (1993, 1994) suggest, the investment ratio is the key control variable in the framework of the economic growth model. The coefficient of $INVEST$ is expected to be positive.

As the indicator of economic openness, we use the ratio of exports and imports to GDP. The data are obtained from the World Bank (2016). Promoting economic openness through trade is thought to increase economic growth (e.g., Frankel and Romer, 1999; Dollar and Kraay, 2004; Freund and Bolaky, 2008; Chang *et al.*, 2009). Therefore, we expect the coefficient of $OPEN$ to be positive.

Finally, we include primary school enrollment to assess educational development. The data are obtained from the World Bank

(2016). Because increased education levels engender human resource development, and thereby economic growth (e.g., Barro, 1991; Mankiw *et al.*, 1992; Sala-i-Martin *et al.*, 2004), the coefficient of SCL is expected to be positive.

1.5 Empirical Technique

For the empirical analysis, we use the dynamic panel model as follows:

$$y_{i,t} = \beta_0 y_{i,t-1} + \beta_{10} x_{i,t} + \beta_{11} x_{i,t-1} + \gamma' Z_{i,t} + \alpha_i + u_{i,t}, \qquad (1.7)$$

where $y_{i,t}$ refers to the dependent variable for region i in year t, and if $|\beta_0| < 1$, it is stationary; $x_{i,t}$ is the explanatory variable whose first-order lag is also a regressor; $Z_{i,t}$ represents the vector of other exogenous variables; α_i is a region-specific fixed effect; and $u_{i,t}$ is the error term. Furthermore, we assume that all explanatory variables are independent of $u_{i,t}$.

To estimate the dynamic panel model, we use the dynamic panel generalized method of moments (GMM) estimator proposed by Arellano and Bond (1991). This method takes the first differences of each model to eliminate fixed effects and then applies GMM to the first-difference models using valid instruments. The GMM estimator optimally exploits all of the linear moment restrictions that follow from the assumption of no serial correlation in the error and uses the level of lagged variables as instruments for the first-difference explanatory variables (Arellano and Bond, 1991). We can deal with the endogeneity problem using the GMM estimator. Moreover, because substantial variation among the sampled regions causes the problem of heteroskedasticity, robust standard errors are estimated.[3]

1.6 Empirical Results

Tables 1.3 and 1.4 report the *J*-statistics and their *p*-values. This test is known as the test for over-identifying restrictions or Hansen's

---

[3]The initial GDP level of each country plays the role of the individual term in the dynamic panel model.

Table 1.3   **Empirical Results (Financial Inclusion)**

	Case 1	Case 2	Case 3	Case 4
$GDP\ (-1)$	0.118	0.281	0.123	0.405
	(0.000)	(0.000)	(0.000)	(0.000)
$FI1$	0.028	0.026		
	(0.000)	(0.000)		
$FI1\ (-1)$		−0.006		
		(0.028)		
$FI2$			0.009	0.015
			(0.000)	(0.000)
$FI2\ (-1)$				−0.006
				(0.028)
$INVEST$	−0.001	−0.003	−0.002	−0.002
	(0.314)	(0.057)	(0.151)	(0.206)
$OPEN$	0.005	0.005	0.004	0.004
	(0.000)	(0.000)	(0.000)	(0.000)
SCL	0.002	0.001	0.008	0.004
	(0.411)	(0.456)	(0.000)	(0.015)
J-statistic	50.725	49.357	58.221	49.827
	(0.226)	(0.234)	(0.074)	(0.220)
Number of cross-sections	148	148	148	148
Sample size	932	932	932	932

Notes: *P*-values are in parentheses and are calculated using robust standard errors. For Case 1, the following instrumental variables for GMM are used: dynamic panel instruments are GDP_{t-j}, $(j = 1, 2, \ldots)$; other instruments are $\Delta FI1_{t-1}$, $\Delta INVEST_{t-1}$, $\Delta OPEN_{t-1}$, and ΔSCL_{t-1}. For Case 2, the following instrumental variables for GMM are used: dynamic panel instruments are GDP_{t-j}, $(j = 1, 2, \ldots)$; other instruments are $\Delta FI1_{t-1}$, $\Delta INVEST_{t-1}$, $\Delta OPEN_{t-1}$, and ΔSCL_{t-1}. For Case 3, the following instrumental variables for GMM are used: dynamic panel instruments are GDP_{t-j}, $(j = 1, 2, \ldots)$; other instruments are $\Delta FI2_{t-1}$, $\Delta INVEST_{t-1}$, $\Delta OPEN_{t-1}$, and ΔSCL_{t-1}. For Case 4, the following instrumental variables for GMM are used: dynamic panel instruments are GDP_{t-j}, $(j = 1, 2, \ldots)$; other instruments are $\Delta FI2_{t-1}$, $\Delta INVEST_{t-1}$, $\Delta OPEN_{t-1}$, and ΔSCL_{t-1} (Δ denotes the first-difference values).

J-test (Hansen, 1982). If the model is specified correctly, then the statistic has a chi-squared distribution asymptotically. As clarified in Tables 1.3 and 1.4, the specifications are not rejected in any case at the 5% significant level. Therefore, the model specifications are supported empirically.

Table 1.4   Empirical Results (Financial Deepening)

	Case 5	Case 6	Case 7	Case 8
GDP (-1)	0.315	0.449	0.220	0.576
	(0.000)	(0.000)	(0.000)	(0.000)
$FD1$	0.413	0.394		
	(0.000)	(0.000)		
$FD1$ (-1)		-0.067		
		(0.004)		
$FD2$			0.294	0.278
			(0.000)	(0.000)
$FD2$ (-1)				-0.143
				(0.000)
$INVEST$	0.006	0.004	0.002	-0.002
	(0.000)	(0.000)	(0.017)	(0.022)
$OPEN$	0.002	0.002	0.002	0.002
	(0.000)	(0.000)	(0.000)	(0.000)
SCL	0.001	0.001	0.004	0.001
	(0.161)	(0.383)	(0.000)	(0.139)
J-statistic	49.374	47.937	56.622	44.883
	(0.267)	(0.279)	(0.096)	(0.393)
Number of cross-sections	91	91	91	91
Sample size	577	577	577	577

Notes: *P*-values are in parentheses and are calculated using robust standard errors. For Case 5, the following instrumental variables for GMM are used: dynamic panel instruments are GDP_{t-j}, $(j = 1, 2, \ldots)$; other instruments are $\Delta FD1_{t-1}$, $\Delta INVEST_{t-1}$, $\Delta OPEN_{t-1}$, and ΔSCL_{t-1}. For Case 6, the following instrumental variables for GMM are used: dynamic panel instruments are GDP_{t-j}, $(j = 1, 2, \ldots)$; other instruments are $\Delta FD1_{t-1}$, $\Delta INVEST_{t-1}$, $\Delta OPEN_{t-1}$, and ΔSCL_{t-1}. For Case 7, the following instrumental variables for GMM are used: dynamic panel instruments are GDP_{t-j}, $(j = 1, 2, \ldots)$; other instruments are $\Delta FD2_{t-1}$, $\Delta INVEST_{t-1}$, $\Delta OPEN_{t-1}$, and ΔSCL_{t-1}. For Case 8, the following instrumental variables for GMM are used: dynamic panel instruments are GDP_{t-j}, $(j = 1, 2, \ldots)$; other instruments are $\Delta FD2_{t-1}$, $\Delta INVEST_{t-1}$, $\Delta OPEN_{t-1}$, and ΔSCL_{t-1} (Δ denotes the first-difference values).

Table 1.3 presents the estimation results of the dynamic panel model for the cases of financial inclusion. In Cases 1 and 2, we use the number of commercial bank branches per $1{,}000 \, \text{km}^2 (FI1)$, and in Cases 3 and 4, the number of commercial bank branches per 100,000 adults ($FI2$) as the measures of financial inclusion. Cases 1 and 3 report the results excluding the one-lagged value of financial inclusion as the explanatory variable, whereas Cases 2 and 4 report the results including the one-lagged value of financial inclusion as the explanatory variable.

First, the coefficients of financial inclusion (FI) are positive as expected and statistically significant at the 1% level in all four cases (0.028 for Case 1, 0.026 for Case 2, 0.009 for Case 3, and 0.015 for Case 4). The coefficients of the one-lagged value of financial inclusion are estimated to be negative and statistically significant in Cases 2 and 4 (-0.006 for Cases 2 and 4). However, the sum of these coefficients is positive in both cases ($0.026 - 0.006 = 0.020$ for Case 2 and $0.015 - 0.006 = 0.009$ for Case 4). The results are robust with respect to the choice of measures of financial inclusion and control variables. Thus, improving the accessibility of financial services leads to increased economic activities among households and companies that face funding constraints. As Rutherford (2000) points out, poor people need access to financial services much more than rich people do, simply because poor people have little money. Such services help poor people manage risks, smooth consumption, take advantage of profitable economic opportunities, and thereby improve their living standards.

Regarding the control variables, Table 1.3 shows that the coefficients of the investment ratio ($INVEST$) are statistically insignificant in all cases. These results suggest that the effect of investment on economic growth is not empirically supported. Next, the coefficients of economic openness ($OPEN$) are estimated to be 0.005 for Cases 1 and 2, and 0.004 for Cases 3 and 4. All these estimates are statistically significant. Thus, increased economic openness positively affects economic growth. Finally, we consider the effect of education on economic growth. The coefficients of the primary school enrollment ratio (SCL) are statistically significant at the 5% level in two out of four cases, suggesting that higher education levels may promote economic growth.

In summary, Table 1.3 shows that increased access to finance and an increase in economic openness promote economic growth.

Table 1.4 presents the estimation results of the dynamic panel model for the cases of financial deepening. In Cases 5 and 6, we use the logarithm of money and quasi-money (M2) as a percentage of GDP ($FD1$), and in Cases 7 and 8, the logarithm of domestic credit by banks to the private sector as a percentage of GDP ($FD2$) as the measures of financial deepening. Cases 5 and 7 report the results excluding the one-lagged value of financial deepening as the explanatory variable, whereas Cases 6 and 8 report the results including the one-lagged value of financial deepening as the explanatory variable.

First, the coefficients of financial deepening (FD) are positive as expected and statistically significant in all four cases (0.413 for Case 5, 0.394 for Case 6, 0.294 for Case 7, and 0.278 for Case 8). The coefficients of the one-lagged value of financial deepening are estimated to be negative and statistically significant in Cases 6 and 8 (-0.067 for Case 6 and -0.143 for Case 8). However, the sum of these coefficients is positive in both cases ($0.394 - 0.067 = 0.327$ for Case 6 and $0.278 - 0.143 = 0.135$ for Case 8). These results indicate that financial sector growth has increased economic growth. The results are robust with respect to the choice of measures of financial deepening and control variables.

Regarding the control variables, Table 1.4 shows that the coefficients of the investment ratio ($INVEST$) are estimated to be positive in three cases (0.006 for Case 5, 0.004 for Case 6, and 0.002 for Case 7) and statistically significant. However, we obtain a negative estimate for Case 8. Therefore, we obtain mixed results for the effect of increased investment on economic growth when we use the variables of financial deepening. Next, the coefficients of economic openness ($OPEN$) are estimated to be 0.002 and statistically significant in all cases. Thus, a rise of economic openness positively influences economic growth. These results are consistent with the results presented in Table 1.3. Finally, we assess the effect of education on economic growth. The coefficients of the primary school enrollment ratio (SCL) range from 0.001 to 0.004. These estimates are not statistically significant at the 5% level in three out of four cases. Therefore, we can infer that a higher education level does not positively affect economic growth.

In summary, Table 1.4 shows that increased financial deepening and an increase in economic openness promote economic growth.

1.7   Concluding Remarks

By estimating panel data from 168 countries between 2004 and 2014, this study empirically analyzed whether financial inclusion through improved access to formal financial services has contributed to economic growth. The estimation results indicate that there is a positive relationship between the number of commercial bank branches and real per capita GDP. Although expanding the network of branches and improving accessibility for customers might be costly for commercial banks in the private sector, improved financial access has the effect of gradually promoting economic growth and enriching people's lives. Therefore, countries should support their banking sectors to increase the penetration of financial services and eliminate barriers to access while maintaining balance between profitability and the public interest.

Furthermore, we found that financial deepening has a positive and significant effect on economic growth in the sample countries. This result suggests that, in addition to financial sector outreach, an expanding financial sector can contribute to growing the economies of these countries.

References

Allen, F., Carletti, E., Cull, R., Qian, J. Q., Senbet, L., Valenzuela, P., 2014. The African financial development and financial inclusion gaps. World Bank Policy Research Working Paper 7019, World Bank, Washington D.C.

Apergis, N., Filippidis, I., Economidou, C., 2007. Financial deepening and economic growth linkages: A panel data analysis. *Review of World Economics* 143, 179–198.

Arellano, M., Bond, S., 1991. Some tests of specification for panel data: Monte Carlo evidence and an application to employment equations. *The Review of Economic Studies* 58, 277–297.

Barro, R. J., 1991. Economic growth in a cross section of countries. *The Quarterly Journal of Economics* 106, 407–443.

Beck, T., 2008. The econometrics of finance and growth. World Bank Policy Research Working Paper 4608, World Bank, Washington D.C.

Beck, T., 2012. The role of finance in economic development: Benefits, risks, and politics, in: Mueller, D. C. (Eds.), *The Oxford Handbook of Capitalism.* Oxford University Press, Oxford, pp. 161–203.

Beck, T., Demirgüç-Kunt, A., Martínez Pería, M. S., 2008. Banking services for everyone? Barriers to bank access and use around the world. *The World Bank Economic Review* 22, 397–430.

Chang, R., Kaltani, L., Loayza, N. V., 2009. Openness can be good for growth: The role of policy complementarities. *Journal of Development Economics* 90, 33–49.

Claessens, S., 2006. Access to financial services: A review of the issues and public policy objectives. *The World Bank Research Observer* 21, 207–240.

De Long, B. J., Summers, L. H., 1993. How strongly do developing economies benefit from equipment investment? *Journal of Monetary Economics* 32, 395–415.

De Long, B. J., Summers, L. H., 1994. How robust is the growth-machinery nexus? in: Baldassarri, M., Paganetto, L., Phelps, E. S. (Eds.), *International Differences in Growth Rates: Market Globalization and Economic Areas.* Palgrave Macmillan, Basingstoke, pp. 5–54.

Demetriades, P. O., Hussein, K. A., 1996. Does financial development cause economic growth? Time-series evidence from 16 countries. *Journal of Development Economics* 51, 387–411.

Demirgüç-Kunt, A., Klapper, L., 2012a. Measuring financial inclusion: The global Findex database. World Bank Policy Research Working Paper 6025, World Bank, Washington D.C.

Demirgüç-Kunt, A., Klapper, L., 2012b. Financial inclusion in Africa: An overview. World Bank Policy Research Working Paper 6088, World Bank, Washington D.C.

Demirgüç-Kunt, A., Maksimovic, V., 1996. Financial constraints, uses of funds, and firm growth: An international comparison. World Bank Policy Research Working Paper 1671, World Bank, Washington D.C.

Dollar, D., Kraay, A., 2004. Trade, growth, and poverty. *The Economic Journal* 114, F22–F49.

Ellis, K., Lemma, A., Rud, J.-P., 2010. Investigating the impact of access to financial services on household investment. Overseas Development Institute Working Paper 4985, Overseas Development Institute, London.

Frankel, J. A., Romer, D., 1999. Does trade cause growth? *American Economic Review* 89, 379–399.

Freund, C., Bolaky, B., 2008. Trade, regulation, and income. *Journal of Development Economics* 87, 309–321.

Graff, M., 2003. Financial development and economic growth in corporatist and liberal market economies. *Emerging Markets Finance and Trade* 39, 47–69.

Hansen, L. P., 1982. Large sample properties of generalized method of moments estimators. *Econometrica* 50, 1029–1054.

Inoue, T., Hamori, S., 2016. Financial access and economic growth: Evidence from sub-Saharan Africa. *Emerging Markets Finance and Trade* 52, 743–753.

International Monetary Fund (IMF), 2016. *Financial Access Survey.* IMF, Washington D.C., http://fas.imf.org/, Accessed 23 January 2016.

King, R. G., Levine, R., 1993. Finance and growth: Schumpeter might be right. *The Quarterly Journal of Economics* 108, 717–737.

Kirkpatrick, C., 2000. Financial development, economic growth, and poverty reduction. *The Pakistan Development Review* 39, 363–388.

Levine, R., 2005. Finance and growth: Theory and evidence, in: Aghion, P., Durlauf, S. N. (Eds.), *Handbook of Economic Growth.* Elsevier, Amsterdam, pp. 865–934.

Levine, R., Renelt, D., 1992. A sensitivity analysis of cross-country growth regressions. *American Economic Review* 82, 942–963.

Levine, R., Zervos, S., 1998. Stock markets, banks and economic growth. *American Economic Review* 88, 537–558.

Luintel, K. B., Khan, M., 1999. A quantitative reassessment of the finance-growth nexus: Evidence from a multivariate VAR. *Journal of Development Economics* 60, 381–405.

Mankiw, N. G., Romer, D., Weil, D. N., 1992. A contribution of the empirics of economic growth. *The Quarterly Journal of Economics* 107, 407–437.

Mialou, A., Amidzic, G., Massara, A., 2017. Assessing countries' financial inclusion standing — A new composite index. *Journal of Banking and Financial Economics* 2, 105–126.

Rebelo, S. T., 1991. Long-run policy analysis and long-run growth. *Journal of Political Economy* 99, 500–521.

Romer, P. M., 1986. Increasing returns and long-run growth. *Journal of Political Economy* 94, 1002–1037.

Rutherford, S., 2000. *The Poor and Their Money.* Oxford University Press, New Delhi.

Sala-i-Martin, X., Doppelhofer, G., Miller, R. I., 2004. Determinants of long-term growth: A Bayesian averaging of classical estimates (BACE) approach. *American Economic Review* 94, 813–835.

Solow, R. M., 1956. A contribution to the theory of economic growth. *The Quarterly Journal of Economics* 70, 65–94.

World Bank, 2016. *World Development Indicators.* World Bank, Washington D.C., http://databank.worldbank.org/data/source/world-development-indicators, Accessed 23 January 2016.

Chapter 2

Financial Inclusion and Poverty Reduction: Has Microfinance Been Helpful to Poor People?[*]

2.1 Introduction

Based on the close relationship between financial development and economic growth, several studies have investigated the putative positive correlation between poverty reduction and increased formal financial activities, citing the elimination of credit constraints on poor people and an increase in their productive assets and productivity (World Bank, 2001; Jalilian and Kirkpatrick, 2002). Indeed, recent econometric studies define financial development as financial deepening and suggest that financial deepening helps reduce poverty both directly and indirectly through its effect on economic growth (e.g., Honohan, 2004; Jalilian and Kirkpatrick, 2005; Beck *et al.*, 2007; Quartey, 2008; Jeanneney and Kpodar, 2011; Inoue and Hamori, 2012).

Unlike these studies, this chapter especially focuses on financial inclusion and empirically examines whether, and to what extent, financial inclusion through microfinance institutions (MFIs) contributes to alleviating poverty in developing countries. Poor people generally lack sufficient collateral and credit history. They have little or no access to basic formal financial services provided by

---

[*]This chapter is a revised version of Inoue and Hamori (2013) that was published in *Applied Financial Economics*. We would like to extend our sincere appreciation to Taylor & Francis for kindly agreeing to include this chapter in this book.

traditional intermediaries. Beginning with small-scale, non-collateral loans in South Asia and Latin America in the 1970s, microfinance has increasingly serviced poor people and the microfinance market has grown considerably in developing countries. Because microfinance generally targets poor people who lack sufficient collateral and credit history, it is one of the few financial intermediary channels available to low-income households. Therefore, the notion of financial inclusion is best embodied by the expansion of microfinance activities in developing countries.

The remainder of this chapter is organized as follows. Section 2.2 reviews the relevant literature on microfinance, especially its effects on poverty and income inequality at the macro level. Section 2.3 presents the models and Section 2.4 explains the definitions, sources, and properties of the data. Section 2.5 shows the empirical results, while Section 2.6 summarizes the main findings of this study and offers several interpretations.

2.2   Literature Review

Over the past few decades, numerous empirical studies have been undertaken to shed light on how microfinance activities affect the well-being of poor people. Although such studies have mainly used sample survey data at the village level, differences in the selected regions, types and amounts of data collected, and empirical methods have meant that opinion remains divided on the effect of microfinance on poverty reduction. For example, Pitt and Khandker (1998), Mosley (2001), and Khandker (2005) all conclude that microcredit increases the incomes of and/or consumption by poor borrowers, although Coleman (1999), Morduch (1999), and Roodman and Morduch (2009) do not.[1,2] From these micro-level case studies, it

---

[1] A positive effect of microfinance on poverty is found in Bangladesh (Pitt and Khandker, 1998; Khandker, 2005) and Bolivia (Mosley, 2001).

[2] In addition, Banerjee *et al.* (2009) and Karlan and Zinman (2009) conclude that the effects of microcredit on borrowers vary depending on client characteristics and that they are not as significant as those claimed by microfinance movement proponents.

remains unclear whether microfinance improves the general welfare of poor people in developing countries.

In light of this lack of consensus, a few empirical analyses have begun to examine the effects of microfinance on poverty and income inequality using multi-country data. For example, Honohan (2008) constructs a composite indicator of financial access for 162 countries by combining information about the number of accounts at commercial banks and at MFIs with household surveys for a smaller set of countries. Using cross-country data, the author compares the composite indicator with the poverty headcount ratio and reports that financial access is negatively correlated with poverty conditions, but that the correlation loses significance in multiple regressions that include per capita income.

Kai and Hamori (2009) examine the effect of microfinance intensity on income inequality using cross-sectional data of 61 developing countries. The authors measure the degree of microfinance intensity using both the number of MFIs and the number of borrowers from MFIs. By regressing the Gini index on microfinance intensity and a set of control variables, including real per capita GDP and its squared term, Kai and Hamori (2009) find that microfinance intensity in terms of the number of MFIs or borrowers from MFIs has a significant negative relationship with income inequality. The authors also find that per capita GDP is estimated to be significantly positive and that its square term is estimated to be significantly negative, which supports Kuznets's inverted-U hypothesis. Based on this evidence, the authors conclude that poor countries should emphasize the equalizing effect of microfinance because economic growth increases inequality before a country's income reaches a certain level.

Imai *et al.* (2012) analyze the poverty-reducing effect of microfinance using cross-sectional data of 48 developing countries for 2007 and panel data of 61 countries for 2003 and 2007. The authors use three poverty indexes: poverty headcount ratio, poverty gap, and squared poverty gap. In their empirical models, each poverty measure is explained in terms of MFIs' gross loan portfolio per capita as well as control variables, such as real per capita GDP, domestic credit as a proportion of GDP, and regional dummies. The authors estimate the models by application of the instrumental variables and ordinary least squares methods. Controlling for the effects of other factors influencing poverty, the authors find that MFIs' gross loan portfolio has a statistically significant negative relationship with all poverty measures.

This study differs from the cited studies in the following three ways. First, we empirically analyze how financial inclusion through MFIs influences poverty in developing countries. The degree of financial inclusion is measured using two indicators: the number of MFIs divided by the population in a country and the number of active borrowers from MFIs divided by the population in a country. Furthermore, we assume that the scaling up of MFIs can serve as a proxy for financial deepening and measure it using the gross loan portfolio of MFIs divided by the population in a country.

Second, we use the poverty ratio as the dependent variable, which is defined as the percentage of people below the poverty line in each country, and its logit transformation value. Using the logit transformation, the poverty ratio, which is usually restricted to values between 0 and 1, is transformed to yield values from minus infinity to plus infinity, thereby satisfying one of the assumptions of standard regression analysis. This is the first study to apply this transformation method to the poverty ratio.

Finally, unlike studies that have adopted cross-country datasets, we use panel data from 76 developing countries, which has the advantage of incorporating the time dimension, and apply the instrumental variable estimation to the panel data in order to overcome potential endogeneity in the equation.

2.3   Models

We conduct a panel analysis of 76 countries using data from 1995 to 2008, with an annual frequency. We empirically analyze how financial inclusion or financial deepening affects the poverty ratio. We use the following models for empirical analysis:

$$POV_{i,t} = \alpha_0 + \alpha_1 FI_{i,t} + \alpha_2 X_{i,t} + u_{i,t},$$

$$i = 1, 2, \ldots, N : t = 1, 2, \ldots, T, \tag{2.1}$$

$$POV_{i,t} = \beta_0 + \beta_1 FD_{i,t} + \beta_2 X_{i,t} + u_{i,t},$$

$$i = 1, 2, \ldots, N : t = 1, 2, \ldots, T, \tag{2.2}$$

$$\ln\left(\frac{POV_{i,t}}{1 - POV_{i,t}}\right) = \alpha_0 + \alpha_1 FI_{i,t} + \alpha_2 X_{i,t} + u_{i,t},$$

$$i = 1, 2, \ldots, N : t = 1, 2, \ldots, T, \tag{2.3}$$

and

$$\ln\left(\frac{POV_{i,t}}{1 - POV_{i,t}}\right) = \beta_0 + \beta_1 FD_{i,t} + \beta_2 X_{i,t} + u_{i,t},$$

$$i = 1, 2, \ldots, N : t = 1, 2, \ldots, T, \tag{2.4}$$

where $POV_{i,t}$ is the poverty ratio in country i at time t; $FI_{i,t}$ is financial inclusion through MFIs in country i at time t; $FD_{i,t}$ is financial deepening through MFIs in country i at time t, $X_{i,t}$ is a vector of control variables in country i at time t; and $u_{i,t}$ is the error term in country i at time t. As control variables, we use the measure of economic openness ($OPEN_{i,t}$), the inflation rate ($INF_{i,t}$), the logarithms of real per capita income ($GDP_{i,t}$), the square of the logarithms of real per capita income ($GDP_{i,t}^2$), and the sub-Saharan African dummy variable ($SADUM_{i,t}$).

It is noteworthy that the poverty ratio takes values from 0 to 1. However, we encounter a serious problem by application of standard regression models, which assume that the explained variable takes values from minus infinity to plus infinity. In order to solve this problem, we use the logit transformation of the poverty ratio as follows[3]:

$$y_{i,t} = \ln\left(\frac{POV_{i,t}}{1 - POV_{i,t}}\right). \tag{2.5}$$

If $y_{i,t}$ approaches 0, then the value of $POV_{i,t}$ approaches minus infinity. If $POV_{i,t}$ approaches 1, then the value of $y_{i,t}$ approaches plus infinity. Therefore, because the transformed value takes values from minus infinity to plus infinity, there is no contradiction with the

---

[3]Logistic regression has been applied to various fields of statistical analysis. Hosmer and Lemeshow (2000) and Kleinbaum and Klein (2010) provide some notable examples.

standard assumption of regression. This approach is also useful for checking the robustness of our empirical results.

Finally, in order to address the problem of endogeneity, we use the instrumental variable method to estimate each parameter. The instrumental variables that we use are a constant term and the lagged value of each explanatory variable.

2.4   Data

For the empirical analysis, we use annual observations of the poverty ratio rather than X-year averages or X-year moving averages. Specifically, this is the poverty headcount ratio at the national poverty line (measured as a percentage of the population). We obtain data on the poverty ratios from the World Development Indicators of the World Bank (2010). Furthermore, we use the transformed value of the poverty ratio for the empirical analysis.

Financial inclusion is the most important explanatory variable in this study. This variable is measured using two microfinance indicators: the number of MFIs divided by the population in a country ($FI1$) and the number of active borrowers divided by the population in a country ($FI2$).[4] The data for the number of MFIs and the number of active borrowers are obtained from the Microfinance Information Exchange (MIX) (2010). The population data are obtained from the World Bank (2010). $FI1$ and $FI2$ are closely related but different concepts. $FI1$ measures financial inclusion in terms of access to microfinance, whereas $FI2$ measures financial inclusion in terms of usage of microfinance. Financial inclusion may ease credit constraints imposed on poor people by expanding national microfinance networks and enlarging the flow of financial services, thereby reducing poverty ratios. Accordingly, we expect each coefficient of FI in Equations (2.1) and (2.3) to have a negative value.

We alternatively consider financial deepening (FD) as a traditional concept of financial development. FD assesses the quantity

---

[4]We multiply $FI1$ by 10,000 in order to adjust the unit in our empirical analysis, that is, $FI1$ equals the ratio of the number of MFIs multiplied by 10,000 to the population.

effect of microfinance expansion on poverty alleviation. We measure the degree of financial deepening using the gross loan portfolio of MFIs divided by the population in a country. The data for the gross loan portfolio are obtained from the MIX (2010), while the population data are obtained from the World Bank (2010). As with financial inclusion, financial deepening is thought to contribute to poverty reduction by eliminating credit constraints on poor people and increasing their productive assets and productivity (World Bank, 2001; Jalilian and Kirkpatrick, 2002). Therefore, the coefficients of FD in Equations (2.2) and (2.4) are expected to be negative.

Table 2.1 presents summary statistics for each indicator of financial inclusion and financial deepening and shows that the degrees of inclusion and deepening increase over time. For example, the average of $FI1$ increases from 0.001 in 1995–1996 to 0.010 in 2007–2008, that of $FI2$ increases from 0.001 to 0.022 over the same period, and that of FD increases from 0.519 to 26.642 in the same timeframe.

For the empirical analysis, we use two measures of economic openness as the control variable: the ratio of exports and imports to GDP ($OPEN1$) and the ratio of foreign direct investment (FDI) to GDP ($OPEN2$). These data are obtained from the World Bank (2010). Many theoretical and empirical studies have analyzed how economic openness affects poor people, especially poor people in developing countries. For example, using a large sample of countries, Dollar and Kraay (2004) observe that economic openness measured in terms of trade integration alleviates poverty. However, some scholars have questioned whether international openness actually contributes to poverty reduction (e.g., Wade, 2004; Milanovic, 2005).

We also control for the inflation rate (INF). This value is calculated as the log difference of the consumer price index (CPI), where the value of the year 2005 is standardized to 100. The source of the CPI is the World Bank (2010). High and unpredictable inflation is considered to have a disproportionately negative effect on poor people, because this population has relatively limited access to financial instruments that hedge against inflation and is likely to have

Table 2.1 Summary Statistics for Indicators of Financial Inclusion and Financial Deepening

		1995–1996	1997–1998	1999–2000	2001–2002	2003–2004	2005–2006	2007–2008
FI1	Mean	0.001	0.002	0.002	0.004	0.007	0.010	0.010
	Standard deviation	0.001	0.002	0.002	0.005	0.008	0.011	0.011
FI2	Mean	0.001	0.002	0.003	0.005	0.009	0.016	0.022
	Standard deviation	0.002	0.003	0.005	0.009	0.015	0.023	0.030
FD	Mean	0.519	0.736	1.190	2.271	6.038	13.182	26.642
	Standard deviation	1.244	1.828	2.463	3.927	9.592	19.834	41.055

Notes: $FI1$ indicates the number of MFIs divided by the population of a country (this value is multiplied by 10,000 to adjust the unit). $FI2$ indicates the number of active borrowers divided by the population in a country. FD indicates the gross loan portfolio divided by the population in a country.

Sources: The data for the number of MFIs, the number of active borrowers, and the gross loan portfolio are obtained from the MIX (2010). The data for population are obtained from the World Development Indicators of the World Bank (2010).

a larger share of cash in its small portfolios (Easterly and Fischer, 2001; Holden and Prokopenko, 2001). Indeed, previous empirical studies, such as Romer and Romer (1998) and Easterly and Fischer (2001), generally support this position for a large sample of countries. In line with the literature, we expect inflation to be detrimental to poor people, and therefore expect the coefficient of INF to have a positive sign.

Furthermore, we include the logarithms of real per capita GDP (GDP) and its square (GDP^2) as control variables, which are measured in constant 2000 US dollars. These data are obtained from the World Bank (2010). Theoretically considered, in certain countries, the benefit of economic growth for poor people might be undermined or even offset if growth is accompanied by an increase in income inequality (Jeanneney and Kpodar, 2011). However, empirical evidence does not support the argument that economic growth affects income distribution. For example, Dollar and Kraay (2002) empirically find that incomes of poor people on average rise in proportion to average incomes, suggesting that economic growth typically benefits poor people as much as it benefits everyone else. Moreover, Li *et al.* (1998) observe that income inequality is relatively stable over time within countries, although it varies significantly across countries. Therefore, based on these research results, we assume that economic growth positively influences poverty reduction. The squared term is also included in the equations to consider the nonlinear effect of income on the poverty ratio.

We also include a dummy variable for the sub-Saharan African region $(SADUM)$, which equals 1 if a country belongs to this region and 0 otherwise. Because this region is considered to comprise countries with high poverty rates, we expect this coefficient to have a positive sign.

2.5 Empirical Results

We estimate each model using the generalized method of moments (GMM) in order to adjust for the endogeneity problem (Hansen, 1982). We use a constant term and the lagged value of each explanatory variable as instruments.[5] Tables 2.2 and 2.3 indicate the empirical results for the cases using the poverty ratio and its logit transformation, respectively. These tables show the coefficient estimates with the standard errors in parentheses below. These tables also report the p-values of the Durbin–Wu–Hausman test (Durbin, 1954; Wu, 1973, 1974; Hausman, 1978). The null hypothesis is that explanatory variables are endogenous and the alternative hypothesis is that explanatory variables are exogenous. Tables 2.2 and 2.3 indicate that the null hypothesis of endogeneity is not rejected in every case, which supports the use of GMM.

The empirical results in Table 2.2 clearly show that the coefficients of financial inclusion variables are statistically significant with the expected signs (-1.986 and -2.167 for $FI1$ and -1.579 and -1.546 for $FI2$). Thus, an increase in the degree of financial inclusion through MFIs significantly reduces, and thereby improves, the poverty ratio. These results are robust to changes in the measures of financial inclusion and control variables.

As expected, the coefficients of financial deepening variables (FD) are negative (-0.002) and statistically significant at the 1% level. These results indicate that financial deepening through MFIs leads to poverty reduction. The results are robust with respect to the choice of control variables.

With regard to the control variables, Table 2.2 further shows that the coefficients of economic openness are estimated to be -0.032, -0.016, and -0.020 for the trade to GDP ratio ($OPEN1$) and 0.460, 0.292, and 0.087 for the FDI to GDP ratio ($OPEN2$). Although these estimates indicate mixed findings for the effects of openness on poverty, they are statistically insignificant in all cases. Thus, an increase in the degree of openness to trade and FDI does not seem to affect the poverty ratio significantly. Although Hamori and Hashiguchi (2012) report that an increase in openness leads to an

---

[5]If the instrumental variables do not have large correlations with the endogenous variables, we suffer from the problem of weak instruments (Bound *et al.*, 1995). Thus, we check the correlation between the endogenous and instrumental variables and find that they are strongly correlated.

increase in inequality, our empirical results indicate that such a rise may not lead to a change in the poverty ratio.

Furthermore, we examine the effect of inflation on the poverty ratio. The coefficients of the inflation rate (INF) are estimated to be in the range of 0.133 to 0.203, and they are statistically significant at the 10% level in four out of six cases. Thus, an increase in the inflation rate may increase, and therefore worsen, the poverty ratio.

The coefficients of real per capita income (GDP) are estimated to be in the range of -0.476 to -0.355, and they are statistically significant at the 5% level in every case. Furthermore, the coefficients of the square of real per capita income (GDP^2) are estimated to be in the range of 0.021 to 0.029, and they are statistically significant at least at the 10% level in every case. Thus, as expected, an increase in economic growth reduces, and thereby improves, the poverty ratio, while it seems to have a nonlinear effect on poverty. Finally, although the coefficients of the sub-Saharan African dummy ($SADUM$) are estimated to be positive, they are not statistically significant.[6]

Table 2.3, in which the logit transformation of the poverty ratio is used as the explained variable, indicates that the coefficients of financial inclusion and financial deepening are estimated to be -6.873 and -8.008 for $FI1$, -6.010 and -6.203 for $FI2$, and -0.008 for FD, and all are statistically significant at least at the 10% level. Thus, an increase in the degree of financial inclusion or financial deepening significantly reduces the poverty ratio. These results are consistent with those presented in Table 2.2.

With respect to the control variables, Table 2.3 shows that the coefficients of economic openness are estimated to be -0.221, -0.116, and -0.151 for $OPEN1$ and 0.944, 0.517, and -0.735 for $OPEN2$. However, these estimates are statistically insignificant in all cases. Thus, changes in the degree of economic openness do not significantly affect the poverty ratio. These results are consistent with those

---

[6]We also use the education variable, namely, the secondary school enrollment ratio, in the empirical analysis. We find that the coefficient of financial inclusion is significantly negative in this case as well, which indicates that increased financial inclusion reduces the poverty ratio.

Table 2.2   Empirical Results for Equations (2.1) and (2.2)

	Case 1		Case 2		Case 3		Case 4		Case 5		Case 6	
	Estimate	SE	Estimate	SE	Estimate	SE	Estimate	SE	Estimate	SE	Estimate	SE
Constant	1.812	(0.635)***	2.219	(0.657)***	1.817	(0.624)***	2.071	(0.629)***	1.909	(0.570)***	2.052	(0.582)***
FI1	−1.986	(0.704)**	−2.167	(0.720)***								
FI2					−1.579	(0.551)***	−1.546	(0.558)**				
FD									−0.002	(0.001)***	−0.002	(0.001)***
OPEN1	−0.032	(0.075)			−0.016	(0.057)			−0.020	(0.063)		
OPEN2			0.460	(0.642)			0.292	(0.532)			0.087	(0.646)
INF	0.203	(0.096)**	0.169	(0.088)*	0.179	(0.184)	0.133	(0.168)	0.184	(0.081)**	0.158	(0.083)*
GDP	−0.355	(0.178)**	−0.476	(0.191)**	−0.358	(0.177)**	−0.438	(0.184)**	−0.391	(0.159)**	−0.436	(0.172)**
GDP^2	0.021	(0.013)*	0.029	(0.014)**	0.021	(0.013)*	0.027	(0.013)**	0.024	(0.011)**	0.027	(0.013)**
SADUM	0.024	(0.052)	0.002	(0.048)	0.027	(0.045)	0.016	(0.044)	0.026	(0.048)	0.018	(0.045)
Durbin–Wu–Hausman	0.019		0.017		0.033		0.002		0.017		0.017	
J-statistic	0.218		0.216		0.311		0.321		0.351		0.368	

(*Continued*)

Table 2.2 (*Continued*)

	Case 1		Case 2		Case 3		Case 4		Case 5		Case 6	
	Estimate	SE	Estimate	SE	Estimate	SE	Estimate	SE	Estimate	SE	Estimate	SE
Adjusted R-squared	0.189		0.190		0.171		0.177		0.253		0.241	
Number of observations	87		87		86		86		87		87	

Notes: $FI1$ indicates the number of MFIs divided by the population of a country (this value is multiplied by 10,000 to adjust the unit). $FI2$ indicates the number of active borrowers divided by the population in a country. FD indicates the gross loan portfolio divided by the population in a country. $OPEN1$ indicates the ratio of exports and imports to GDP. $OPEN2$ indicates the ratio of FDI to GDP. INF indicates the inflation rate. GDP and GDP^2 indicate the logarithms of real per capita GDP and its square, respectively. $SADUM$ indicates a dummy variable for the sub-Saharan African region. SE indicates the standard error, which is calculated using the White cross-section SEs and covariance. Numbers in parentheses represent SEs. ***, **, and * indicate statistical significance at the 1%, 5%, and 10% levels, respectively. The row for the Durbin–Wu–Hausman test indicates probability values of this test. J-statistic indicates the probability value of Hansen's J-statistic.

Instrumental variables: Case 1: Constant, $FI1_{i,t-1}$, $OPEN1_{i,t-1}$, $GDP_{i,t-1}$, $GDP_{i,t-2}$, $GDP^2_{i,t-1}$, $GDP^2_{i,t-2}$, $SADUM$. Case 2: Constant, $FI1_{i,t-1}$, $OPEN2_{i,t-1}$, $GDP_{i,t-1}$, $GDP_{i,t-2}$, $GDP^2_{i,t-1}$, $GDP^2_{i,t-2}$, $SADUM$. Case 3: Constant, $FI2_{i,t-1}$, $OPEN1_{i,t-1}$, $GDP_{i,t-1}$, $GDP_{i,t-2}$, $GDP^2_{i,t-1}$, $GDP^2_{i,t-2}$, $SADUM$. Case 4: Constant, $FI2_{i,t-1}$, $OPEN2_{i,t-1}$, $GDP_{i,t-1}$, $GDP_{i,t-2}$, $GDP^2_{i,t-1}$, $GDP^2_{i,t-2}$, $SADUM$. Case 5: Constant, $FD_{i,t-1}$, $OPEN1_{i,t-1}$, $GDP_{i,t-1}$, $GDP_{i,t-2}$, $GDP^2_{i,t-1}$, $GDP^2_{i,t-2}$, $SADUM$. Case 6: Constant, $FD_{i,t-1}$, $OPEN2_{i,t-1}$, $GDP_{i,t-1}$, $GDP_{i,t-2}$, $GDP^2_{i,t-1}$, $GDP^2_{i,t-2}$, $SADUM$.

Table 2.3 Empirical Results for Equations (2.3) and (2.4)

	Case 7		Case 8		Case 9		Case 10		Case 11		Case 12	
	Estimate	SE	Estimate	SE	Estimate	SE	Estimate	SE	Estimate	SE	Estimate	SE
Constant	6.383	(3.338)*	7.379	(3.436)**	6.533	(3.304)*	6.863	(3.254)**	7.065	(2.924)**	6.749	(3.111)**
$FI1$	−6.873	(3.713)*	−8.008	(3.712)**								
$FI2$					−6.010	(2.240)***	−6.203	(2.414)**				
FD									−0.008	(0.003)***	−0.008	(0.003)**
$OPEN1$	−0.221	(0.350)	0.944	(2.540)	−0.116	(0.261)						
$OPEN2$							0.517	(1.929)	−0.151	(0.289)	−0.735	(2.625)
INF	1.205	(0.459)***	1.024	(0.410)**	1.045	(0.942)	0.695	(0.776)	1.082	(0.368)***	0.940	(0.374)**
GDP	−1.693	(0.950)*	−2.009	(0.998)**	−1.755	(0.936)*	−1.889	(0.946)**	−1.920	(0.824)**	−1.856	(0.916)**
GDP^2	0.099	(0.067)	0.121	(0.072)*	0.104	(0.067)	0.114	(0.068)*	0.117	(0.059)*	0.112	(0.066)*
$SADUM$	0.047	(0.236)	−0.001	(0.236)	0.072	(0.217)	0.078	(0.223)	0.046	(0.219)	0.069	(0.220)
Durbin–Wu–Hausman	0.008		0.000		0.015		0.001		0.006		0.000	
J-statistic	0.218		0.216		0.302		0.321		0.323		0.368	

(*Continued*)

Table 2.3 (*Continued*)

	Case 7		Case 8		Case 9		Case 10		Case 11		Case 12	
	Estimate	SE	Estimate	SE	Estimate	SE	Estimate	SE	Estimate	SE	Estimate	SE
Adjusted R-squared	0.214		0.207		0.164		0.177		0.266		0.241	
Number of observations	87		87		86		86		87		87	

Notes: $FI1$ indicates the number of MFIs divided by the population of a country (this value is multiplied by 10,000 to adjust the unit). $FI2$ indicates the number of active borrowers divided by the population in a country. FD indicates the gross loan portfolio divided by the population in a country. $OPEN1$ indicates the ratio of exports and imports to GDP. $OPEN2$ indicates the ratio of FDI to GDP. INF indicates the inflation rate. GDP and GDP^2 indicate the logarithms of real per capita GDP and its square, respectively. $SADUM$ indicates a dummy variable for the sub-Saharan African region. SE indicates the standard error, which is calculated using the White cross-section SEs and covariance. Numbers in parentheses represent SEs. ***, **, and * indicate statistical significance at the 1%, 5%, and 10% levels, respectively. The row for the Durbin–Wu–Hausman test indicates probability values of this test. J-statistic indicates the probability value of Hansen's J-statistic.

Instrumental variables: Case 7: Constant, $FI1_{i,t-1}$, $OPEN1_{i,t-1}$, $GDP_{i,t-1}$, $GDP_{i,t-2}$, $GDP^2_{i,t-1}$, $GDP^2_{i,t-2}$, $SADUM$. Case 8: Constant, $FI1_{i,t-1}$, $OPEN2_{i,t-1}$, $GDP_{i,t-1}$, $GDP_{i,t-2}$, $GDP^2_{i,t-1}$, $GDP^2_{i,t-2}$, $SADUM$. Case 9: Constant, $FI2_{i,t-1}$, $OPEN2_{i,t-1}$, $GDP_{i,t-1}$, $GDP_{i,t-2}$, $GDP^2_{i,t-1}$, $GDP^2_{i,t-2}$, $SADUM$. Case 10: Constant, $FI2_{i,t-1}$, $OPEN2_{i,t-1}$, $GDP_{i,t-1}$, $GDP_{i,t-2}$, $GDP^2_{i,t-1}$, $GDP^2_{i,t-2}$, $SADUM$. Case 11: Constant, $FD_{i,t-1}$, $OPEN1_{i,t-1}$, $GDP_{i,t-1}$, $GDP_{i,t-2}$, $GDP^2_{i,t-1}$, $GDP^2_{i,t-2}$, $SADUM$. Case 12: Constant, $FD_{i,t-1}$, $OPEN2_{i,t-1}$, $GDP_{i,t-1}$, $GDP_{i,t-2}$, $GDP^2_{i,t-1}$, $GDP^2_{i,t-2}$, $SADUM$.

presented in Table 2.2. In addition, the coefficients of the inflation rate (INF) are estimated to be in the range of 0.695 to 1.205, and they are statistically significant in four out of six cases. Thus, a rise in the inflation rate may lead to an increase in the poverty ratio.

Concerning the income effect, the coefficients of real per capita income (GDP) are estimated to be in the range of -2.009 to -1.693, and they are statistically significant at least at the 10% level in every case. Similarly, the coefficients of the square of real per capita income (GDP^2) are estimated to be in the range of 0.099 to 0.121, and they are statistically significant in four out of six cases. Thus, an increase in economic growth reduces, and thereby improves, the poverty ratio, and it may have a nonlinear effect on poverty. Finally, although the coefficients of the sub-Saharan African dummy ($SADUM$) are estimated to be positive, they are not statistically significant. These results are also consistent with those presented in Table 2.2.

In summary, it is clear from Tables 2.2 and 2.3 that financial inclusion, financial deepening, and economic growth improve the poverty ratio. Economic growth may have a nonlinear effect on poverty, whereas the inflation rate may worsen it. With regard to economic openness and the sub-Saharan African regional dummy, we find no significant effect on the poverty ratio.

2.6   Concluding Remarks

The role played by the financial sector in an economy has received much attention, and it has been analyzed in the literature from both theoretical and empirical viewpoints. In particular, in the past few decades, the microfinance sector has exhibited considerable growth to the point that it is increasingly regarded as the most effective tool for stimulating financial development in less developed countries. Therefore, this study specifically investigated whether financial inclusion and financial deepening through microfinance actually alleviate poverty globally.

Because the development of the microfinance sector is considered to benefit poorer populations by expanding national microfinance networks and making more money available to low-income house-holds, we measured the degree of financial inclusion through MFIs using two indicators: the number of MFIs divided by the population in a country and the number of active borrowers divided by the population in a country. We also assumed that the scaling up of MFIs can serve as a proxy for financial deepening and measured it using the gross loan portfolio of MFIs divided by the population in a country. Then, using unbalanced panel data from 76 developing countries between 1995 and 2008, we estimated the models in which the poverty ratio is explained by each indicator of financial inclusion and financial deepening as well as certain control variables. From the panel instrumental variable estimation, we obtained the findings outlined below.

First, financial inclusion through MFIs significantly reduces the poverty ratio, a result that holds true regardless of the indicator of financial inclusion used. In addition, financial deepening through MFIs significantly reduces the poverty ratio. As such, although previous micro-level analyses have not yet agreed on how microfinance affects poverty reduction, this study indicates that the expansion of microfinance activities contributes to alleviating poverty at the macro level. Importantly, our findings are obtained in both cases of the dependent variable (i.e., the poverty ratio and its logit transformation), which reinforces the robustness of these empirically obtained results.

Second, we found that the coefficient of the inflation rate tends to have a significant positive value, whereas the coefficient of real per capita GDP has a significant negative value. These findings suggest that a stable macroeconomic environment, determined by a low inflation rate and/or high economic growth, is a necessary condition for poverty reduction. We also found that economic growth may have a nonlinear effect on poverty.

Third, in contrast to our results obtained for the inflation rate and per capita GDP, economic openness does not have a statistically significant relationship with the poverty ratio. Finally, the coefficient of the sub-Saharan African dummy has a positive sign, but not a statistically significant relationship with the poverty ratio. This result differs from that found in earlier studies conducted using cross-country datasets.

In summary, the presented empirical evidence indicates that financial inclusion indeed contributes to reducing poverty across the world. Some recent empirical studies have already corroborated that the development of the formal financial sector, especially in the banking industry, improves living standards in poorer countries. However, this study presents some of the first pieces of evidence on the positive effect of microfinance expansion on poverty using a worldwide panel dataset. Therefore, these findings suggest that microfinance has a reciprocal relation with formal financial institutions' activities for poverty alleviation. Indeed, there are several examples indicating that the banking sector has become the most important source of funds for promoting the growth of MFIs around the world. Taking the foregoing into account, we conclude that microfinance should be exploited by policymakers and practitioners in developing countries as one of the promising instruments for reducing poverty.

References

Banerjee, A., Duflo, E., Glennerster, R., Kinnan, C., 2009. The miracle of microfinance? Evidence from a randomized evaluation. Mimeo.

Beck, T., Demirgüç-Kunt, A., Levine, R., 2007. Finance, inequality and the poor. *Journal of Economic Growth* 12, 27–49.

Bound, J., Jaeger, D. A., Baker, R. M., 1995. Problems with instrumental variables estimation when the correlation between the instruments and the endogenous explanatory variable is weak. *Journal of the American Statistical Association* 90, 443–450.

Coleman, B. E., 1999. The impact of group lending in northeast Thailand. *Journal of Development Economics* 60, 105–141.

Dollar, D., Kraay, A., 2002. Growth is good for the poor. *Journal of Economic Growth* 7, 195–225.

Dollar, D., Kraay, A., 2004. Trade, growth, and poverty. *The Economic Journal* 114, F22–F49.

Durbin, J., 1954. Errors in variables. *Review of the International Statistical Institute* 22, 23–32.

Easterly, W., Fischer, S., 2001. Inflation and the poor. *Journal of Money, Credit and Banking* 33, 160–178.

Hamori, S., Hashiguchi, Y., 2012. The effect of financial deepening on inequality: Some international evidence. *Journal of Asian Economics* 23, 353–359.

Hansen, L. P., 1982. Large sample properties of generalized method of moments estimators. *Econometrica* 50, 1029–1054.

Hausman, J. A., 1978. Specification tests in econometrics. *Econometrica* 46, 1251–1271.

Holden, P., Prokopenko, V., 2001. Financial development and poverty alleviation: Issues and policy implications for developing and transition countries. IMF Working Paper WP/01/160, International Monetary Fund, Washington D.C.

Honohan, P., 2004. Financial development, growth and poverty: How close are the links? World Bank Policy Research Working Paper 3203, World Bank, Washington D.C.

Honohan, P., 2008. Cross-country variation in household access to financial services. *Journal of Banking and Finance* 32, 2493–2500.

Hosmer, D. W., Lemeshow, S., 2000. *Applied Logistic Regression*, 2nd edn. Wiley-Interscience Publication, New York.

Imai, K. S., Gaiha, R., Thapa, G., Annim, S. K., 2012. Microfinance and poverty — A macro perspective. *World Development* 40, 1675–1689.

Inoue, T., Hamori, S., 2012. How has financial deepening affected poverty reduction in India? Empirical analysis using state-level panel data. *Applied Financial Economics* 22, 395–408.

Inoue, T., Hamori, S., 2013. Financial permeation as a role of microfinance: Has microfinance actually been a viable financial intermediary for helping the poor? *Applied Financial Economics* 23, 1567–1578.

Jalilian, H., Kirkpatrick, C., 2002. Financial development and poverty reduction in developing countries. *International Journal of Finance & Economics* 7, 97–108.

Jalilian, H., Kirkpatrick, C., 2005. Does financial development contribute to poverty reduction? *Journal of Development Studies* 41, 636–656.

Jeanneney, G. S., Kpodar, K., 2011. Financial development and poverty reduction: Can there be a benefit without a cost? *Journal of Development Studies* 47, 143–163.

Kai, H., Hamori, S., 2009. Microfinance and inequality. *Research in Applied Economics* 1, 1–12.

Karlan, D., Zinman, J., 2009. Expanding microenterprise credit access: Using randomized supply decisions to estimate the impacts in Manila. Economic Growth Center Discussion Paper 976, Yale University, New Haven.

Khandker, S. R., 2005. Microfinance and poverty: Evidence using panel data from Bangladesh. *The World Bank Economic Review* 19, 263–286.

Kleinbaum, D. G., Klein, M., 2010. *Logistic Regression: A Self-Learning Text*, 3rd edn. Springer, New York.

Li, H., Squire, L., Zou, H., 1998. Explaining international and intertemporal variations in income inequality. *The Economic Journal* 108, 26–43.

Microfinance Information Exchange (MIX), 2010. *Indicators for Microfinance Institutions*. MIX, Washington D.C., http://www.mixmarket.org/mfi/indicators, Accessed 19 August 2010.

Milanovic, B., 2005. Can we discern the effect of globalization on income distribution? Evidence from household surveys. *The World Bank Economic Review* 19, 21–44.

Morduch, J., 1999. The microfinance promise. *Journal of Economic Literature* 37, 1569–1614.

Mosley, P., 2001. Microfinance and poverty in Bolivia. *Journal of Development Studies* 37, 101–132.

Pitt, M. M., Khandker, S. R., 1998. The impact of group-based credit programs on poor households in Bangladesh: Does the gender of participants matter? *Journal of Political Economy* 106, 958–996.

Quartey, P., 2008. Financial sector development, savings mobilization and poverty reduction in Ghana, in: Guha-Khasnobis, B., Mavrotas, G. (Eds.), *Financial Development, Institutions, Growth and Poverty Reduction.* Palgrave Macmillan, Basingstoke, pp. 87–119.

Romer, C. D., Romer, D. H., 1998. Monetary policy and the well-being of the poor. NBER Working Paper 6793, National Bureau of Economic Research, Cambridge.

Roodman, D., Morduch, J., 2009. The impact of microcredit on the poor in Bangladesh: Revisiting the evidence. CGD Working Paper 174, Center for Global Development, Washington D.C.

Wade, R. H., 2004. Is globalization reducing poverty and inequality? *World Development* 32, 567–589.

World Bank, 2001. *World Development Report 2000/2001: Attacking Poverty.* Oxford University Press, New York.

World Bank, 2010. *World Development Indicators.* World Bank, Washington D.C., http://databank.worldbank.org/data/source/world-development-indicators, Accessed 19 August 2010.

Wu, D.-M., 1973. Alternative tests of independence between stochastic regressors and disturbances. *Econometrica* 41, 733–750.

Wu, D.-M., 1974. Alternative tests of independence between stochastic regressors and disturbances: Finite sample results. *Econometrica* 42, 529–546.

Chapter 3

Remittance Inflows and Economic Growth: Clarifying Conflicting Results in the Literature

3.1 Introduction

The amount of migrants' remittances has increased year after year, especially since the early 2000s, as Figure 3.1 shows. Remittance inflows into developing economies were US$ 0.3 billion in 1970, significantly less than inflows of foreign direct investment (FDI) and official development assistance (ODA), which were US$ 1.9 billion and US$ 5.6 billion, respectively. Since then, remittances have risen steadily to about US$ 49 billion in 1994, for the first time outpacing ODA received. Remittance flows have gained momentum since the early 2000s, reaching US$ 367 billion in 2012. Although this represents less than half the amount of FDI inflows (US$ 898 billion), remittance inflows have grown to approximately four times the amount of ODA (US$ 94 billion) and have become the largest source of external finance for some developing countries, such as India, the Philippines, Nigeria, Egypt, Bangladesh, and Pakistan.[1]

Unlike ODA and FDI, remittances are individual and private unrequited income transfers between overseas workers and their families in their home countries. On the one hand, migrants' remittances

---

[1] Among 101 developing countries for which we could obtain comparative data in 2012, the amount of remittances exceeded the amounts of FDI and ODA in 39 countries.

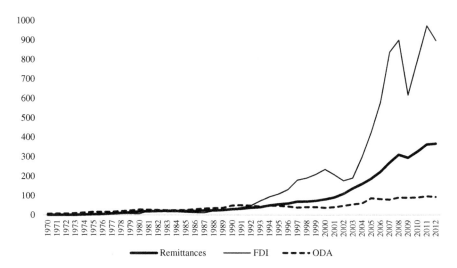

Figure 3.1   Sources of External Financing for Developing Countries (US\$ billion)

Source: World Bank (2014).

might help family members to obtain additional income, enable them to expand consumption, accumulate physical and human capital, and/or increase financial investments (International Monetary Fund (IMF), 2005, p. 72). An increase in remittances, therefore, could be expected to stimulate economic growth and alleviate poverty conditions in remittance-receiving countries. On the other hand, migrants' remittances could detract from economic growth because they tend to be compensatory and countercyclical to the home country's economic condition (Chami *et al.*, 2005, p. 56). Furthermore, remittances might detract from economic activity in the home country by creating disincentives to work among remittance-receiving families and reduce their countries' labor supplies and labor participation rates (*ibid.*, p. 77).[2]

Against the background of a surge in these capital flows, a considerable amount of literature has empirically analyzed whether

---

[2]Moreover, remittances might hamper the receiving country's global competitiveness through appreciation in real exchange rates (Amuedo-Dorantes and Pozo, 2004).

and how remittances affect economic growth in receiving countries. Results have been inconclusive and contradictory. Most studies attribute growth-promoting effects to remittances (Acosta *et al.*, 2008; Calderón *et al.*, 2008; Pradhan *et al.*, 2008; Catrinescu *et al.*, 2009; Giuliano and Ruiz-Arranz, 2009; Mundaca, 2009; Ramirez and Sharma, 2009; Vargas-Silva *et al.*, 2009; Fayissa and Nsiah, 2010; Bettin and Zazzaro, 2012; Cooray, 2012; Nyamongo *et al.*, 2012; Kumar, 2013; Lartey, 2013; Nsiah and Fayissa, 2013; Ramirez, 2013; Abida and Sghaier, 2014; Goschin, 2014; Imai *et al.*, 2014; Chowdhury, 2016; Meyer and Shera, 2017).[3]

However, other empirical analyses find a negative effect of remittances on growth (Chami *et al.*, 2005; Barajas *et al.*, 2009; Singh *et al.*, 2011), an insignificant effect (IMF, 2005; Jongwanich, 2007; Rao and Hassan, 2011; Koyame-Marsh, 2012; Senbeta, 2013; Adams and Klobodu, 2016), or neither a causal nor a long-run relationship between remittances and growth (Ahamada and Coulibaly, 2013; Lim and Simmons, 2015).

This study reinvestigates these mixed findings by considering the cumulative effects of remittances on economic growth in developing countries. Controlling for several potential growth determinants, we estimate models in which real per capita GDP is explained by remittances and their squared term, the use of which suggests that the growth-promoting effect of remittances might change nonlinearly across thresholds. If the coefficient of remittances has a positive (negative) sign and their squared term has a negative (positive) sign, the remittances–growth relationship takes an inverted U-shape (U-shape).

The empirical analysis uses unbalanced panel data for 130 developing countries from 1995 to 2013. In estimating the models, we adopt panel cointegration tests, dynamic ordinary least squares (DOLS), and fully modified ordinary least squares (FMOLS). We

---

[3]Imai *et al.* (2014) indicate that remittance inflows have been beneficial to economic growth, but that the volatility of remittances has been harmful to economic growth.

believe ours is the first study to examine the remittances–growth relationship in developing countries using these methods.

This chapter is organized as follows. Section 3.2 reviews the relevant literature. Section 3.3 presents our model and provides the definitions, sources, and properties of the data. Section 3.4 explains the empirical techniques. Section 3.5 presents the empirical results. Section 3.6 summarizes the major findings.

3.2   Literature Review

Several studies have been conducted so far to analyze the remittances–growth nexus. Table 3.1 summarizes the related empirical studies on the effect of remittances on economic growth. As this table shows, most studies have supported a positive and significant effect of remittances on growth in developing countries. For example, Catrinescu *et al.* (2009) explore whether remittances affect economic growth and whether institutional quality influences the effect of remittances on growth. The authors use a panel dataset for 162 developing countries from 1970 to 2003. Their results indicate that remittances and the interaction term between remittances and institutions have significant positive coefficients, suggesting that remittances enhance macroeconomic growth and that their effect is greater in countries with sound policies and higher-quality institutions.

Giuliano and Ruiz-Arranz (2009) verify that financial deepening in recipient countries influences the effect of remittances on economic growth. Employing the ordinary least squares (OLS) and system generalized method of moments (GMM) techniques using data for 73 developing countries spanning 1975–2002, the authors estimate models in which the real per capita GDP growth is explained by remittances, financial deepening, and their interaction term. Giuliano and Ruiz-Arranz (2009) find significant positive coefficients of remittances and financial deepening and a negative coefficient of their interaction term. These findings suggest that remittances support economic growth in countries with less developed financial systems by providing an alternative source for financing investment.

Vargas-Silva *et al.* (2009) analyze whether remittances boost economic growth in Asia using panel data for 26 developing countries between 1988 and 2007. Their model is a growth regression, including remittances, remittances squared, and a set of control variables, and is estimated by OLS, fixed-effects, and random-effects methods, respectively. The authors report that the positive effect of remittances is significant in fixed-effects and random-effects estimations, although remittances squared have a significant negative coefficient only in the fixed-effects estimation. Therefore, the authors indicate that the relationship between remittances and economic growth can be nonlinear and that there is a threshold beyond which the contribution of remittances to growth diminishes in Asian developing countries.

Bettin and Zazzaro (2012) examine the effects of the relationship between remittances and financial development on economic growth for 66 developing countries from 1970 (or 1991) to 2005. The authors proxy financial development using either the size or the inefficiency of the banking sector. From the OLS and system GMM estimations, the authors find that the coefficients of remittances are positive and statistically significant, whereas the interaction terms for remittances and size/efficiency of the banking sector correlate negatively and positively, respectively, with real per capita GDP. Bettin and Zazzaro (2012) conclude that remittances enhance economic growth in countries with highly efficient and small banking sectors.

By contrast, several empirical analyses have demonstrated that remittances have a negative and/or insignificant effect on economic growth. For example, Chami *et al.* (2005) investigate whether remittances are a source of capital for economic development similar to FDI and other private capital flows. Using data for 113 countries spanning 1970–1998, the authors estimate models in which the real per capita GDP growth is explained by either remittances or a change in remittances and control variables. Results from cross-sectional and panel estimations document a robust negative relationship between the per capita GDP growth and the growth rate of remittances, suggesting remittances are compensatory in nature and countercyclical with respect to income in migrants' home countries.

Table 3.1   Summary of Literature on the Remittances — Growth Nexus

Author(s)	Countries Period	Variables	Method(s)	Results
Chami *et al.* (2005)	113 countries 1970–1998	*Dependent variable:* the log difference of real per capita GDP *Independent variables:* (1) the logarithm of worker remittances to GDP ratio or its log difference, the logarithm of initial value of real per capita GDP, the logarithm of investment to GDP ratio, net private capital flows to GDP ratio, regional dummies (2) the log difference of worker remittances to GDP ratio, the logarithm of investment to GDP ratio, net private capital flows to GDP ratio, inflation rate, regional dummies	(1) OLS, Cross-country (2) Common slope or Fixed effects, Panel	There is a robust negative correlation between the growth rate of remittances and per capita GDP growth. This suggests that remittances are compensatory in nature and that remittances do not act like a source of capital for economic development.
IMF (2005)	101 countries 1970–2003	*Dependent variable:* growth of real per capita output *Independent variables:* remittances to GDP ratio, secondary school enrollment ratio,	IV, Cross-country	There is no statistically significant direct link between real per capita output growth and remittances.

(*Continued*)

Table 3.1 (*Continued*)

Author(s)	Countries Period	Variables	Method(s)	Results
		investment to GDP ratio, instruments (geographical distance between home country and host country, the presence of a common language in home countries and host countries)		(1) The direct effect of remittances on economic growth is negative and statistically insignificant.
Jongwanich (2007)	17 countries in Asia and the Pacific 1993–2003 (3-year average)	*Dependent variable:* (1) growth of real per capita GDP (2) real gross fixed capital formation as a share of GDP (3) human development index *Independent variables:* (1) remittances as a share of GDP, the initial level of real per capita GDP, real gross fixed capital formation as a share of GDP, human development index, goods exports and goods imports to total output ratio, real government consumption as a share of GDP, inflation rate	(1) (2) System GMM, Panel (3) Fixed effects-IV, Panel	(2) (3) The estimated coefficients of remittances are positive and statistically significant. In summary, remittances can operate positive effects on economic growth in Asia and the Pacific countries through investment and human capital channels, but their effects are marginal.

(*Continued*)

Table 3.1   (*Continued*)

Author(s)	Countries Period	Variables	Method(s)	Results
		(2) remittances as a share of GDP, growth of real per capita GDP, lagged real gross fixed capital formation as a share of GDP, goods exports and goods imports to total output ratio, inflation rate, real interest rate (3) remittances as a share of GDP, the initial level of real per capita GDP All variables are transformed into logarithms.		
Acosta *et al.* (2008)	67 countries	*Dependent variable:* change in per capita income *Independent variables:* lagged remittances as a percentage of GDP, lagged per capita income, investment as a percentage of GDP, secondary school enrollment ratio, private domestic credit to GDP ratio, International Country	Panel	Remittances have a positive and significant effect on economic growth and this effect is robust to the use of external and time varying instrumental variables to control for the potential endogeneity of remittances. However, the magnitude of the estimated

(*Continued*)

Table 3.1 (*Continued*)

Author(s)	Countries Period	Variables	Method(s)	Results
		Risk Guide (ICRG) political risk index, real exports and imports to GDP ratio, inflation rate, real exchange rate overvaluation, general government consumption All variables are transformed into logarithms.		effect of remittances on growth is relatively small in economic terms. Moreover, when domestic investment is included as an additional explanatory variable, the effect of remittances on growth ceases to be significant. This may imply that one of the main channels through which remittances affect economic growth is by increasing domestic investment.
Calderón *et al.* (2008)	N/A	*Dependent variable:* change in per capita income *Independent variables:* remittances (workers remittances to GDP ratio), lagged per capita income, primary or secondary	GMM-IV, Panel	The growth benefits of remittances rise as the level of human capital increases. The marginal effect of remittances is higher for countries with higher levels

(*Continued*)

Table 3.1 (*Continued*)

Author(s)	Countries Period	Variables	Method(s)	Results
		school enrollment ratio, ICRG political risk index, private domestic credit to GDP ratio, real exports and imports to GDP ratio, inflation rate, real exchange rate overvaluation, general government consumption, the interaction term (remittances and primary or secondary school enrollment ratio, remittances and ICRG political risk index, remittances and private domestic credit to GDP ratio, or remittances and policy index) All variables are transformed into logarithms.		of institutional quality. Remittances promote growth, but the effect declines as the financial system becomes deeper. Remittances are more effective in enhancing growth prospects in countries with better economic policies.
Pradhan *et al.* (2008)	39 developing countries 1980–2004	*Dependent variable:* change in real per capita GDP *Independent variables:* real remittances per capita, lagged per capita GDP, investment to	Fixed effects, Panel	Remittances have a positive effect on economic growth although the effect is not very large in size and the coefficient of the remittances' variable is

(*Continued*)

Table 3.1 (*Continued*)

Author(s)	Countries Period	Variables	Method(s)	Results
		GDP ratio, exports and imports to GDP ratio or exports to GDP ratio, political regime index or its lagged value All variables are transformed into logarithms. All independent variables are averages for 5-year periods.		significant in two of four models. Since official estimates of remittances used in this analysis tend to understate actual numbers considerably, more accurate data on remittances is likely to reveal an even more pronounced effect of remittances on economic growth.
Barajas *et al.* (2009)	84 countries 1970–2004	*Dependent variable:* growth of real per capita GDP *Independent variables:* the fitted value from a first-stage regression of remittances (the logarithm of workers' remittances to GDP ratio) and/or its squared, the interaction term between remittances and M2 to GDP ratio,	OLS-IV or Fixed effects-IV, Panel	Remittances have a statistically significant effect on growth in less than half of the estimations, and when they have a significant effect, it is generally negative. Therefore, there is no robust evidence that remittances have made the

(Continued)

Table 3.1 (*Continued*)

Author(s)	Countries Period	Variables	Method(s)	Results
		the trade-weighted average growth rate of real per capita GDP of the remittance-receiving country's top 20 trading partners		sort of contribution to economic growth.
Catrinescu *et al.* (2009)	162 countries 1970–2003	*Dependent variable:* change in per capita GDP *Independent variables:* remittances (workers' remittances to GDP ratio), lagged change in per capita GDP, gross capital formation to GDP ratio, net private capital flows to GDP ratio, institution index, the interaction term between remittances and institution index All variables except for institution index are transformed into logarithms.	GMM, Panel	The results indicate that remittances appear to have a positive and statistically significant effect on economic growth in five out of nine cases. The effect of remittances appears to be more positive when controlling for the potential endogeneity bias in remittances and considering remittances in conjunction with institutional variable. Remittances' effect on growth is higher in countries that have higher-quality policies and institutions.

(*Continued*)

Table 3.1 (*Continued*)

Author(s)	Countries Period	Variables	Method(s)	Results
Giuliano and Ruiz-Arranz (2009)	73 developing countries 1975–2002 (5-year average)	*Dependent variable:* growth of real per capita GDP *Independent variables:* remittances (remittances to GDP ratio), financial deepening (the ratio of currency plus demand and interest bearing liabilities of banks and non-bank financial intermediaries to GDP, the ratio of demand, time, saving, and foreign currency deposits to GDP, the ratio of claims on the private sector to GDP, or the ratio of credit provided by the banking sector to GDP), the interaction term between remittances and financial deepening, the initial level of real per capita GDP, inflation rate, goods exports and goods imports to total output ratio, the average number of years of secondary schooling,	OLS or System GMM, Panel	They find a positive and significant coefficient of remittance inflows and a negative interaction between remittances and financial deepening. These findings suggest that the marginal effect of remittances on economic growth is decreasing with the level of financial deepening. In other words, remittances have contributed to promote economic growth in countries with shallower financial systems.

(*Continued*)

Table 3.1 (*Continued*)

Author(s)	Countries Period	Variables	Method(s)	Results
		central government fiscal balance to GDP ratio, gross fixed capital formation to GDP ratio, population growth All variables except for inflation rate and central government fiscal balance to GDP ratio are transformed into natural logarithms.		
Mundaca (2009)	25 countries in Latin American and the Caribbean 1970–2002	*Dependent variable:* growth of per capita output *Independent variables:* lagged remittances as a percentage of GDP, lagged growth of per capita output, lagged domestic private credit provided by the banking sector as a share of GDP, the logarithm of gross fixed capital formation per capita, literacy rate, population growth	Difference GMM, Panel	When the indicator of the degree of financial market development together with remittances enter in the growth equation, the corresponding parameter of financial intermediation becomes much more significant statistically and/or numerically, and remittances have a stronger positive effect on economic

(*Continued*)

Table 3.1 (*Continued*)

Author(s)	Countries Period	Variables	Method(s)	Results
				growth. Therefore, remittances enhance further economic growth if financial markets are well developed, and these two together can accelerate growth and remove financing constraints on both firms' and individuals' development.
Ramirez and Sharma (2009)	23 countries in Latin American and the Caribbean 1990–2005	*Dependent variable:* change in the logarithm of real per capita GDP *Independent variables:* remittances (the logarithm of remittances as a percentage of GDP), financial deepening (credit provided by the banking sector to GDP ratio), the interaction term between	Cointegration tests, FMOLS, Panel	Remittances have a positive and significant effect on economic growth. The effect is more pronounced when the financial deepening variable is included. The sign of the coefficient of the interaction term between remittances and domestic credit

(*Continued*)

Table 3.1 (*Continued*)

Author(s)	Countries Period	Variables	Method(s)	Results
		remittances and financial deepening, lagged change in the logarithm of real per capita GDP, fixed capital formation, exports and imports to GDP ratio, labor force		is negative, implying that remittances can act as a substitute for financial deepening.
Vargas-Silva *et al.* (2009)	26 countries in Asia 1988–2007	*Dependent variable:* growth of per capita GDP *Independent variables:* remittances as a percentage of GDP and its squared, the initial level of per capita GDP, primary school completion rate, gross capital formation as a percentage of GDP, inflation rate, exports and imports as a percentage of GDP All variables except for the primary school completion rate and inflation rate are transformed into natural logarithms.	OLS, Fixed effects, or Random effects, Panel	Remittances positively affect home country real per capita GDP growth. A 10% increase in remittances as a share of GDP leads to a 0.9–1.2% increase in GDP growth. The results suggest that remittances can help spur short-term fluctuations in output in Asia.

(*Continued*)

Table 3.1 (*Continued*)

Author(s)	Countries Period	Variables	Method(s)	Results
Fayissa and Nsiah (2010)	36 countries in Africa 1980–2004	*Dependent variable:* real per capita GDP *Independent variables:* remittances per capita, gross fixed capital formation as a percentage of real GDP, gross secondary and tertiary school enrollment ratios, ODA, FDI as a percentage of GDP, other official flows, the ratio of the export to import price indices, economic freedom index, the initial level of real per capita GDP, GDP divided by the product of gross capital formation and labor force All variables are transformed into natural logarithms.	Random effects, Quasi fixed effects, or Dynamic GMM, Panel	Remittances have a positive and statistically significant effect on per capita GDP. A 10% increase in remittances of a typical African country would result in about 0.4% increase in average per capita income.

(*Continued*)

Table 3.1   (*Continued*)

Author(s)	Countries Period	Variables	Method(s)	Results
Rao and Hassan (2011)	40 countries 1965–2004 (5-year average)	*Dependent variable:* growth of real per capita GDP *Independent variables:* remittances, the initial level of real per capita GDP, money and quasi-money, general government final consumption expenditure, inflation rate, exports and imports of goods and services, gross domestic fixed investment, FDI, capital stock All variables are transformed into logarithms. All independent variables except for the initial level of real per capita GDP, inflation rate, and capital stock are expressed as the ratio to GDP.	System GMM, Panel	The coefficients of remittances are negative and insignificant. When reestimating the equation by removing investment and monetary aggregates, the coefficient of remittances is negative and significant. Therefore, it is difficult to conclude that remittances have any long-run permanent and direct growth effects. Remittances may have some indirect and permanent growth effects through its effects on the channels like investment and monetary aggregates, although these indirect growth effects are likely to be small.

(*Continued*)

Table 3.1 (*Continued*)

Author(s)	Countries Period	Variables	Method(s)	Results
Singh *et al.* (2011)	36 countries in sub-Saharan Africa 1990–2008	*Dependent variable:* change in real per capita GDP *Independent variables:* remittances (remittances to GDP ratio), lagged real per capita GDP, investment to GDP ratio, financial deepening (domestic credit provided by banks as a percentage of GDP or money and quasi-money as a percentage of GDP), population growth, institutional quality index, real exchange rate, government expenditure to GDP ratio, exports and imports to GDP ratio, inflation rate, change in export price index to import price index ratio, the interaction term between remittances and institutional quality index, the interaction term between remittances and financial deepening All variables are transformed into logarithms.	Fixed effects 2SLS, Panel	The effect of remittances on economic growth is negative and significant, whether or not interaction terms or a measure for financial deepening is included. Regressions without interaction terms indicate that a 1% rise in the remittances-to-GDP ratio would reduce the per capita GDP growth rate by about 0.015%.

(*Continued*)

Table 3.1 *(Continued)*

Author(s)	Countries Period	Variables	Method(s)	Results
Bettin and Zazzaro (2012)	66 developing countries (1) 1970–2005 (5-year average) (2) 1991–2005 (annual or 5-year average)	*Dependent variable:* growth of real per capita GDP *Independent variables:* (1) remittances (remittances to GDP ratio), financial deepening (the ratio of liquid liabilities of the financial system to GDP, the ratio of domestic credit provided by the banking sector to GDP, the ratio of bank deposits to GDP, or the ratio of claims on the private sector to GDP), the interaction term between remittances and financial deepening, control variables (the initial level of real per capita GDP, the logarithm of gross fixed capital formation to GDP ratio, population growth, inflation rate, central	OLS or System GMM, Panel	(1) When the interaction term is included, remittances appear to promote growth in countries where the size of the financial sector is small and access to external credit for receiving families is very limited. (2) When bank inefficiency indicator is considered to measure the quality of the banking sector, remittances have a positive effect on economic growth only if the domestic banking system is sufficiently sound.

(Continued)

Table 3.1 (*Continued*)

Author(s)	Countries Period	Variables	Method(s)	Results
		government final expenditure to GDP ratio, the logarithm of exports and imports to GDP ratio, institutional quality index) (2) remittances, financial deepening, bank inefficiency, the interaction term between remittances and bank inefficiency, and/or the interaction between remittances and institutional quality index, the same control variables as (1)		Therefore, the size of the domestic banking sector and its efficiency have opposite effects on the development potential of remittances.
Cooray (2012)	Six countries in South Asia 1970–2008	*Dependent variable:* growth of real per capita output *Independent variables:* remittances (remittances to GDP ratio), exports to GDP ratio, FDI to GDP ratio, M2 to GDP ratio, government expenditure to GDP	OLS, Fixed effects, or System GMM, Panel	The coefficients of remittances are positive and statistically significant in all cases, suggesting that remittances contribute to economic growth in South Asia. The coefficients of the

(*Continued*)

Table 3.1 (*Continued*)

Author(s)	Countries Period	Variables	Method(s)	Results
		ratio, human capital (gross secondary school enrollment ratio), physical capital (capital per capita), the interaction terms (remittances and human capital, remittances and physical capital, and remittances and M2 to GDP ratio) All variables are transformed into natural logarithms.		interaction terms between remittances and human capital and between remittances and M2 to GDP ratio are positive and statistically significant. Therefore, remittances act to increase economic growth through the enrollment ratio and financial deepening in South Asia.
Koyame-Marsh (2012)	ECOWAS 10 countries 1976–2003	*Dependent variable:* real GDP growth *Independent variables:* remittances to GDP ratio, FDI inflows to GDP ratio, total external debt to GDP ratio, gross domestic investment to GDP ratio, exports to GDP ratio, the initial level of per capita GDP, error correction term	OLS, Time series	The estimated coefficients of remittances are statistically insignificant in all countries except for Benin. In Benin, the estimated coefficient of remittances is negative and statistically significant.

(*Continued*)

Table 3.1 (*Continued*)

Author(s)	Countries Period	Variables	Method(s)	Results
		All variables except for the initial level of per capita GDP are transformed to their first difference.		
Nyamongo *et al.* (2012)	36 countries in Africa 1980–2009 (3-year average)	*Dependent variable:* growth of real per capita GDP *Independent variables:* remittances (remittances to GDP ratio), standard deviation of remittances, financial deepening (the ratio of credit to the private sector to GDP or the ratio of broad money supply to GDP), the interaction term between remittances and financial deepening, lagged real per capita GDP, gross investment to GDP ratio, inflation rate, gross primary school enrollment ratio, total government expenditure to GDP ratio, exports and imports to GDP ratio	OLS or 2SLS, Panel	Remittances are important in explaining economic growth in African countries. There is a negative relationship between volatility of remittances and economic growth, although this evidence is not strong as some of the estimated coefficients are not found to be statistically significant. Remittances appear to be working as a complement to financial deepening. However, the importance of financial deepening in boosting economic growth appears weakened among the countries under study.

(*Continued*)

Table 3.1 (*Continued*)

Author(s)	Countries Period	Variables	Method(s)	Results
Ahamada and Coulibaly (2013)	20 countries in sub-Saharan Africa 1980–2007	(1) real remittances per capita, real per capita GDP, real per capita US GDP (2) real remittances per capita, real gross fixed capital formation per capita, real per capita US GDP All variables are transformed into logarithms.	Granger causality test	(1) There is no causality between remittances and economic growth in the sample countries. (2) There is no causality from remittances to physical capital investment in all countries except for Gambia. In Gambia, there is a positive causality from remittances to investment. These results point out that remittances do not increase GDP growth because remittances are not used to make capital investment.

(*Continued*)

Table 3.1   (*Continued*)

Author(s)	Countries Period	Variables	Method(s)	Results
Kumar (2013)	Guyana 1982–2010	*Dependent variable:* real per worker output *Independent variables:* workers' remittances as a percentage of GDP, domestic credit to the private sector as a percentage of GDP, real capital stock per worker, net ODA as a percentage of GDP All variables are transformed into logarithms.	(1) ARDL, Time series (2) Granger causality test, Time series	(1) Remittances have a positive and significant effect on economic growth both in the short and the long run. (2) Capital stock, ODA, and financial deepening cause remittance inflows.
Lartey (2013)	36 countries in sub-Saharan Africa 1990–2008	*Dependent variable:* growth of per capita GDP *Independent variables:* remittances, financial deepening (private credit, bank assets, or M2), the interaction term between remittances and financial deepening, investment, government expenditure, exports and imports, population growth, inflation rate	Dynamic GMM, Panel	There is a positive relationship between remittances and per capita GDP growth, and a positive interaction effect between remittances and financial deepening. Therefore, the effect of remittances on economic growth is positive and increases with the level of financial deepening.

(*Continued*)

Table 3.1   (*Continued*)

Author(s)	Countries Period	Variables	Method(s)	Results
		All variables except for growth of per capita GDP and inflation rate are transformed into logarithms. All independent variables except for population growth and inflation rate are expressed as a percentage of GDP.		
Nsiah and Fayissa (2013)	64 countries (29 from Africa, 14 from Asia, and 21 from Latin America and the Caribbean) 1985–2007	*Dependent variable:* real per capita GDP *Independent variables:* remittances per capita, trade as a percentage of GDP, gross fixed capital formation divided by labor force, freedom index	FMOLS, Panel	Remittances have a positive and significant long-run effect on economic growth for the regions as a group and in each of the three regions. Comparatively, a 10% increase in remittances lead to a 0.10%, 1.56%, 0.29%, and 0.13% long-run growth in Africa, Asia, Latin America and the Caribbean, and all regions, respectively. Therefore,

(*Continued*)

Table 3.1 (*Continued*)

Author(s)	Countries Period	Variables	Method(s)	Results
				remittances contribute more to the long-run per capita growth in Asia than in the other regions, suggesting that there are differences in the transmission costs and uses of remittances for economic growth in the recipient regions.
Ramirez (2013)	23 countries in Latin America and the Caribbean (13 lower-income countries and 10 upper middle-income countries) 1990–2007	*Dependent variable:* change in the logarithm of real per capita GDP *Independent variables:* remittances (the logarithm of remittances as a percentage of GDP), lagged change in the logarithm of real per capita GDP, financial deepening (credit provided by the banking sector as a percentage of GDP), fixed capital formation as a percentage of GDP,	FMOLS, Panel	In the lower-income countries, remittances and financial deepening have a positive and significant effect on economic growth. Meanwhile, In the upper middle-income countries, remittances have a positive and significant effect on growth, while financial deepening has a negative effect on growth. In both groups, the interaction

(*Continued*)

Table 3.1   (*Continued*)

Author(s)	Countries Period	Variables	Method(s)	Results
		exports and imports to GDP ratio, labor force, economic freedom index, the interaction term between remittances and financial deepening, the interaction term between remittances and economic freedom index		term between remittances and financial deepening has a negative and significant coefficient, implying that remittances act as substitutes for financial deepening.
Senbeta (2013)	50 countries 1970–2004 (5-year average)	*Dependent variable:* (1) gross capital formation (2) TFP growth (3) growth of real per capita GDP *Independent variables:* (1) remittances, financial deepening (the logarithm of domestic credit to the private sector), lagged gross capital formation, gross domestic savings, FDI inflows, growth of real per capita GDP, exports and imports, the logarithm of general government final consumption expenditure,	OLS, Fixed effects, Fixed effects-IV, or System GMM, Panel	(1) Remittances have a consistently significant positive effect on investment. (2) Remittances have no statistically significant effect on TFP growth. (3) Remittances have no statistically significant effect on economic growth. Therefore, remittances have a conflicting effect on the sources of economic growth.

(Continued)

Table 3.1 (*Continued*)

Author(s)	Countries Period	Variables	Method(s)	Results
		ODA, inflation rate, political risk rating index		
		(2) remittances, financial deepening, the initial level of TFP, exports and imports, the logarithm of general government final consumption expenditure, ODA, inflation rate, political risk rating index, the interaction term between remittances and financial deepening		
		(3) remittances, financial deepening, lagged real per capita GDP, gross capital formation, exports and imports, ODA, inflation rate, political risk rating index, the interaction term between remittances and financial deepening		

(*Continued*)

Table 3.1 (*Continued*)

Author(s)	Countries Period	Variables	Method(s)	Results
		All independent variables except for TFP, real per capita GDP, inflation rate, and political risk rating index are expressed as a percentage of GDP.		The coefficients of remittances are positive and statistically significant, suggesting that remittances significantly contribute to economic growth in North Africa.
Abida and Sghaier (2014)	Four countries in North Africa 1980–2011	*Dependent variable:* growth of real per capita GDP *Independent variables:* remittances to GDP ratio, financial deepening (liquid liabilities of the financial system divided by GDP or bank credit divided by GDP), the interaction term between remittances and financial deepening, control variables (inflation rate, exports and imports to GDP ratio, gross fixed capital formation to GDP ratio, central government expenditures to GDP ratio, lagged per capita GDP) All control variables except for growth of per capita GDP and inflation rate are transformed into natural logarithms.	System GMM, Panel	The coefficients of financial deepening are positive and statistically significant. The coefficients of the interaction term are positive and statistically significant, indicating that remittances contribute to economic growth through its interaction with financial deepening.

(*Continued*)

Table 3.1 (*Continued*)

Author(s)	Countries Period	Variables	Method(s)	Results
Goschin (2014)	10 countries in Central and Eastern Europe 1996–2011	*Dependent variable:* (1) the logarithm of real GDP (2) GDP growth *Independent variables:* (1) the logarithm of lagged real remittances, the logarithm of labor force, the logarithm of real gross fixed capital formation, the logarithm of high-technology exports, the logarithm of lagged real FDI net inflows (2) remittances as a percentage of GDP, population growth, gross fixed capital formation as a percentage of GDP, trade as a percentage of GDP, lagged FDI net inflows as a percentage of GDP, labor force with tertiary education as a percentage of total labor force, lagged research and development	Fixed effects, Panel	Remittances have the significant positive influence on both real GDP and its growth.

(*Continued*)

Table 3.1 (*Continued*)

Author(s)	Countries Period	Variables	Method(s)	Results
		expenditure as a percentage of GDP, employment in services as a percentage of total employment, change in real labor productivity per person employed		
Imai *et al.* (2014)	24 countries in Asia and the Pacific (1) 1980–2009 (annual) (2) 1980–2009 (5-year average)	*Dependent variable:* growth of real per capita GDP *Independent variables:* (1) the logarithm of remittances as a percentage of GDP, the logarithm of deposit money bank assets as a share of deposit money and central bank assets, lagged real per capita GDP, inflation rate, internal armed conflicts, fuel exports as percentage of merchandise exports, capital account openness index, the logarithm of gross capital formation as a percentage of GDP	(1) Fixed effects, Random effects, or 2SLS, Panel (2) VAR, Panel	(1) Remittances have been beneficial to economic growth in Asia. The coefficient estimate ranges from 1.078 (0.805) in case of fixed (random) effects model to 1.702 (1.196) in case of fixed (random) 2SLS model. (2) The volatility of remittances and FDI is harmful to economic growth. The coefficient estimates indicate that the negative effects of volatility are little larger

(*Continued*)

Table 3.1 (*Continued*)

Author(s)	Countries Period	Variables	Method(s)	Results
		(2) the logarithm of real per capita GDP, the standard deviation of remittances, the standard deviation of FDI		with FDI than with remittances.
Lim and Simmons (2015)	13 countries in the Caribbean Community and Common Market region 1975–2010	real per capita GDP, real per capita investment, real per capita consumption, real per capita remittances, 5-year average of real per capita GDP, trade to GDP ratio, financial deepening (domestic credit as a percentage of GDP or money and quasi money as a percentage of GDP)	Cointegration tests, Panel	There is no evidence for the long-run relationship between per capita remittances and per capita GDP. However, there is some evidence for the relationship between per capita remittances and per capita consumption. Therefore, remittance inflows into this region are used for consumption purposes.

(*Continued*)

Table 3.1   (*Continued*)

Author(s)	Countries Period	Variables	Method(s)	Results
Adams and Klobodu (2016)	33 countries in sub-Saharan Africa 1970–2012 (5-year average)	*Dependent variable:* growth of real per capita GDP *Independent variables:* remittances, lagged real per capita GDP, regime type, regime durability, the interaction term between remittances and regime type, the interaction term between remittances and regime durability, exports, net FDI inflows, M2, government expenditure, gross secondary school enrollment ratio All variables are transformed into logarithms. All variables except for real per capita GDP, regime type, regime durability, and gross secondary school enrollment ratio are expressed as a percentage of GDP.	System GMM, Panel	Remittances do not have a robust effect on economic growth. However, the coefficients of the interaction terms between remittances and regime type and between remittances and regime durability are positive and statistically significant. Therefore, the growth effect of remittances is stimulated in the presence of democratic and stable governments.

(*Continued*)

Table 3.1 (*Continued*)

Author(s)	Countries Period	Variables	Method(s)	Results
Chowdhury (2016)	33 developing countries 1979–2011	*Dependent variable:* GDP growth *Independent variables:* remittances, financial deepening (domestic credit to the private sector to GDP ratio, total domestic credit provided by the banking sector to GDP ratio, M2 to GDP ratio, or M3 to GDP ratio), lagged GDP growth, growth of gross capital formation, the size of the population in the age group 16–64 years, GDP growth in high-income OECD countries and China, ODA, other external flows, the interaction term between remittances and financial deepening	Two-step GMM, Panel	There is a positive and significant relationship between remittances and GDP growth. However, the effect of financial deepening on remittances is insignificant. In addition, the interaction term between remittances and financial deepening is insignificant. Therefore, financial deepening neither works as a substitute nor a complement for the remittances–growth nexus.

(*Continued*)

Table 3.1   (*Continued*)

Author(s)	Countries Period	Variables	Method(s)	Results
Meyer and Shera (2017)	Six countries in South Eastern Europe 1999–2013	*Dependent variable:* the natural logarithm of per capita GDP *Independent variables:* remittances, gross fixed capital formation, household final consumption expenditure, the logarithm of secondary school enrollment ratio, the terms of trade, population growth, real exchange rate, government debt All independent variables except for real exchange rate are expressed as a percentage of GDP.	Fixed effects, Panel	Remittances have a positive effect on economic growth and this effect increases at higher levels of remittances relative to GDP.

Barajas *et al.* (2009) introduce an instrument for remittances and a control variable that were not used in previous studies of remittances' growth-promoting effects. The authors construct the ratio of remittances to GDP of all other recipient countries as an alternative instrument, and complement it with the trade-weighted average growth rate of real per capita GDP among the remittance-receiving country's top 20 trading partners. Barajas *et al.*'s (2009) estimations apply OLS and fixed-effects instrumental variable regressions to panel data for 84 recipient countries from 1970 to 2004. The authors report that remittances have negative signs in most cases and that, when the full set of control variables is used, remittances tend to have positive but insignificant coefficients.

In addition, the IMF (2005) and Singh *et al.* (2011) indicate insignificant and negative effects of remittances on economic growth, respectively. The IMF (2005) applies instrumental variable methods to a sample of up to 101 countries from 1970 to 2003 and finds no statistically significant relationship between real per capita output growth and remittances. Using 1990–2008 panel data for 36 countries in sub-Saharan Africa and employing a fixed-effects two-stage least squares (2SLS) estimation, Singh *et al.* (2011) indicate that remittances exert negative and significant effects on economic growth.

3.3 Model and Data

As mentioned in the previous section, most studies attribute growth-promoting effects to remittances. However, several studies demonstrate that remittances have a negative or insignificant effect on economic growth and that, even when it is positive, the effect might diminish gradually. To shed light on these findings, we add remittances squared as an important regressor and examine how the growth effect of remittances varies over time. The model is specified as follows:

$$GDP_{i,t} = \beta_0 + \beta_1 REM_{i,t} + \beta_2 REM_{i,t}^2 + \beta_3 INVEST_{i,t}$$
$$+ \beta_4 OPEN_{i,t} + \beta_5 SCL_{i,t} + u_{i,t},$$
$$i = 1, 2, \ldots, N; \quad t = 1, 2, \ldots, T. \tag{3.1}$$

Here, $GDP_{i,t}$ is the logarithmic value of real per capita GDP in country i during period t. $REM_{i,t}$ is personal remittances as a ratio of GDP in country i during period t. $REM_{i,t}^2$ is the square value of $REM_{i,t}$. $INVEST_{i,t}$ is the investment ratio in country i during period t. $OPEN_{i,t}$ is the measure of economic openness in country i during period t. $SCL_{i,t}$ is the measure of human capital formation in country i during period t. $\beta_0, \beta_1, \beta_2, \beta_3, \beta_4$, and β_5 are unknown parameters. $u_{i,t}$ is the error term.

As the most important independent variables, linear and quadratic terms of remittances (REM and REM^2) are included in Equation (3.1). Since the literature has not yet shown consensus about the effect of remittances on economic growth, we cannot *a priori* predict the signs of linear and quadratic terms of remittances in Equation (3.1). If the coefficient of REM in Equation (3.1) has a positive (negative) sign and the coefficient of REM^2 in Equation (3.1) has a negative (positive) sign, the remittances–growth relationship takes an inverted U-shape (U-shape).

With regard to the control variables, we consider the investment ratio ($INVEST$), economic openness ($OPEN$), and school enrollment ratio (SCL) in Equation (3.1). The investment ratio is a fundamental determinant of economic growth in neoclassical and endogenous growth models. We include this variable to capture the effect of physical capital formation on real per capita GDP. Representative works by Levine and Renelt (1992), Mankiw *et al.* (1992), and De Long and Summers (1991, 1993) empirically find a robust positive relationship between the investment ratio and per capita growth, although these studies identify no causal directionality. In line with these studies, we expect that the increase in investment ratio revitalizes economic activity and that the coefficient of $INVEST$ in Equation (3.1) is positive.

As a control variable, we use a typical indicator of economic openness, namely, the ratio of exports and imports to GDP ($OPEN$). Openness through international trade is considered to promote growth by improving specialization and efficient resource allocation according to comparative advantage, facilitating technology and knowledge transfer, and increasing domestic competition through

Table 3.2   Definition and Source of Each Variable

Variable	Definition	Source
GDP	Logarithm of real per capita GDP (constant 2005 US$)	
REM	Personal remittances, received, as a percentage of GDP	World
INVEST	Gross capital formation as a percentage of GDP	Bank
OPEN	Exports and imports of goods and services as a percentage of GDP	(2014)
SCL	Gross primary school enrollment ratio, both sexes (%)	

international competition (Sachs and Warner, 1995). Several studies empirically show that greater trade openness engenders higher economic growth (Dollar, 1992; Sachs and Warner, 1995; Edwards, 1998; Frankel and Romer, 1999; Dollar and Kraay, 2004). Therefore, the coefficient of *OPEN* in Equation (3.1) is expected to be positive.

Finally, we include education measured by the primary school enrollment ratio (*SCL*) as a control variable. Increased education enables the workforce to absorb, develop, and adopt new technology, in turn aiding technological progress and economic growth (Krueger and Lindahl, 2001; Barro, 2013). Therefore, the coefficient of *SCL* in Equation (3.1) is expected to be positive.

We use panel data of annual data from 1995 to 2013 for 130 countries. All data are obtained from the World Development Indicators of the World Bank (2014). Table 3.2 shows the definition and source of each variable.

3.4   Empirical Techniques

3.4.1   *Panel Cointegration Analysis*

This study adopts the Johansen–Fisher-type panel cointegration tests developed by Maddala and Wu (1999) and follows a two-step approach.

In the first step, two types of cointegration tests, proposed by Johansen (1988) and Johansen and Juselius (1990), are run for each panel data. This procedure shows the probability values $P_{\text{trace},i}$ and $P_{\text{max},i}$ obtained from the trace test and the maximum eigenvalue test, respectively. In the second step, two statistics for the full panel along with $\lambda_{\text{trace},p}$ and $\lambda_{\text{max},p}$ are calculated using the following equations:

$$\lambda_{\text{trace},p} = -2 \sum_{i=1}^{N} \ln P_{\text{trace},i}, \tag{3.2}$$

$$\lambda_{\text{max},p} = -2 \sum_{i=1}^{N} \ln P_{\text{max},i}. \tag{3.3}$$

Both $\lambda_{\text{trace},p}$ and $\lambda_{\text{max},p}$ have a χ^2 distribution with $2N$ degrees of freedom.

3.4.2   *Panel Cointegration Estimation: FMOLS and DOLS*

To estimate the cointegrating vector, Phillips and Hansen (1990) propose a single-equation method based on OLS with semi-parametric correction for serial correlation and endogeneity, which is FMOLS. Let the dependent variable be denoted by y_t and the vector of regressors by x_t, where x_t is a $m \times 1$ vector and $t = 1, 2, \ldots, T$. The behavior of y_t and x_t is assumed to satisfy

$$y_t = x_t'\beta + d_t'\alpha + u_{1t}, \tag{3.4}$$

$$x_t = x_{t-1} + u_{2t}, \tag{3.5}$$

where d_t is a vector of deterministic trend regressors. Let $u_t = (u_{1t}, u_{2t}')'$ be a joint innovation process. Then, the one-sided long-run covariance matrix Λ and long-run covariance matrix Ω can be expressed, respectively, as

$$\Lambda = \sum_{i=0}^{\infty} E(u_t u_{t-i}') = \begin{bmatrix} \lambda_{11} & \lambda_{12} \\ \lambda_{21} & \Lambda_{22} \end{bmatrix}, \tag{3.6}$$

$$\Omega = \sum_{i=-\infty}^{\infty} E(u_t u_{t-i}') = \begin{bmatrix} \omega_{11} & \omega_{12} \\ \omega_{21} & \Omega_{22} \end{bmatrix}. \tag{3.7}$$

Let $y_t^{+} = y_t - \hat{\omega}_{12}\hat{\Omega}_{22}^{-1}\Delta x_t$ and $\hat{\lambda}_{12}^{+} = \hat{\lambda}_{12} - \hat{\omega}_{12}\hat{\Omega}_{22}^{-1}\hat{\Lambda}_{22}$, where $\hat{\lambda}_{12}$, $\hat{\omega}_{12}$, $\hat{\Omega}_{22}^{-1}$, and $\hat{\Lambda}_{22}$ are consistent estimates of the respective parameters. The FMOLS estimator is given by

$$\begin{bmatrix} \hat{\beta} \\ \hat{\alpha} \end{bmatrix} = \left(\sum_{t=1}^{T} z_t z_t' \right)^{-1} \left(\sum_{t=1}^{T} z_t y_t^+ - T \begin{bmatrix} \hat{\lambda}_{12}^{+'} \\ 0 \end{bmatrix} \right), \qquad (3.8)$$

where $z_t = (x_t', d_t')'$.

Saikkonen (1992) and Stock and Watson (1993) propose DOLS as a simple efficient estimator. DOLS specification simply adds leads and lags of the first differences of stochastic regressors to the standard cointegrating regression.

$$y_t = x_t'\beta + d_t'\alpha + \sum_{i=-K}^{K} \Delta x_{t+i}'\gamma + v_t. \qquad (3.9)$$

Obtained from Equation (3.9), the DOLS estimator $(\hat{\beta}', \hat{\alpha}')'$ has the same asymptotic distribution as those obtained via FMOLS.

3.5   Empirical Results

3.5.1   *Panel Cointegration Tests*

The results of the Johansen–Fisher-type panel cointegration tests are shown in Table 3.3 for the system of (GDP, REM, REM^2, $INVEST$, $OPEN$, and SCL). Under the null hypothesis of no cointegration, the trace test statistic (p-value) is 766.100 (0.000), and the maximum eigenvalue test statistic (p-value) is 476.700 (0.000) for the system. The null hypothesis is rejected in both cases, and we find that there is a single cointegration relationship among variables. Therefore, the logarithm of per capita GDP and other variables move together in the long run.

Table 3.3   Panel Cointegration Tests (GDP, REM, REM^2, $INVEST$, $OPEN$, and SCL)

H_0	H_A	Test statistic	p-value
Fisher statistic from the trace test			
$r = 0$	$r \geq 1$	766.100	0.000
Fisher statistic from the maximum eigenvalue test			
$r = 0$	$r = 1$	476.700	0.000

Note: r is the number of cointegration vectors.

3.5.2   *Panel Cointegration Estimation*

The final step is to estimate the cointegration equation using FMOLS and DOLS. Table 3.4 indicates the estimation results of the system (GDP, REM, REM^2, $INVEST$, $OPEN$, and SCL). The coefficient of remittances (REM) is estimated to be positive (0.0203 for FMOLS and 0.0207 for DOLS) and statistically significant at the 1% level. The coefficient of remittances squared (REM^2) is estimated to be negative (-0.0003 for FMOLS and -0.0003 for DOLS) and statistically significant at least at the 5% level.

These results are consistent with those of Vargas-Silva *et al.* (2009), who find that remittances and squared remittances have a positive and a negative effect on economic growth in Asia, respectively. In the analysis, they estimate modes using OLS, fixed-effects, and random-effects estimations and do not check for non-stationarity of data. Our empirical results indicate that their results

Table 3.4   Empirical Results of FMOLS and DOLS (GDP, REM, REM^2, $INVEST$, $OPEN$, and SCL)

Variable	Estimate	p-value
FMOLS		
REM	0.0203	(0.000)
REM^2	−0.0003	(0.000)
$INVEST$	0.0074	(0.000)
$OPEN$	0.0022	(0.000)
SCL	0.0030	(0.000)
Adjusted R-squared	0.981	
Total panel (unbalanced) observations	1,458	
DOLS		
REM	0.0207	(0.000)
REM^2	−0.0003	(0.025)
$INVEST$	0.0088	(0.000)
$OPEN$	0.0026	(0.000)
SCL	0.0028	(0.032)
Adjusted R-squared	0.977	
Total panel (unbalanced) observations	1,150	

are robust to the time-series properties of all the data. In addition, our findings suggest that the nonlinear effect of remittances on economic growth could occur across the developing world as a whole.

With regard to the control variables, the coefficient of the investment ratio (*INVEST*) is estimated to be positive (0.0074 for FMOLS and 0.0088 for DOLS) and statistically significant at the 1% level. In addition, the coefficient of economic openness (*OPEN*) is estimated to be positive (0.0022 for FMOLS and 0.0026 for DOLS) and statistically significant at the 1% level. Furthermore, the coefficient of school enrollment ratio (*SCL*) is estimated to be positive (0.0030 for FMOLS and 0.0028 for DOLS) and statistically significant at least at the 5% level.

3.6 Concluding Remarks

Some relevant studies find a positive effect of remittances on economic growth in developing countries (e.g., Acosta *et al.*, 2008; Calderón *et al.*, 2008; Pradhan *et al.*, 2008; Catrinescu *et al.*, 2009; Giuliano and Ruiz-Arranz, 2009; Mundaca, 2009; Ramirez and Sharma, 2009; Vargas-Silva *et al.*, 2009; Fayissa and Nsiah, 2010; Bettin and Zazzaro, 2012; Cooray, 2012; Nyamongo *et al.*, 2012; Kumar, 2013; Lartey, 2013; Nsiah and Fayissa, 2013; Ramirez, 2013; Abida and Sghaier, 2014; Goschin, 2014; Imai *et al.*, 2014; Chowdhury, 2016; Meyer and Shera, 2017). However, several other empirical studies find a negative effect of remittances on growth (Chami *et al.*, 2005; Barajas *et al.*, 2009; Singh *et al.*, 2011), an insignificant effect (IMF, 2005; Jongwanich, 2007; Rao and Hassan, 2011; Koyame-Marsh, 2012; Senbeta, 2013; Adams and Klobodu, 2016), or neither a causal nor a long-run relationship between remittances and growth (Ahamada and Coulibaly, 2013; Lim and Simmons, 2015). Therefore, the effect of remittances on economic growth has been quantitatively inconclusive.

Considering the different findings in relevant studies, we include remittances squared as a regressor to allow for the nonlinear effect of remittances on economic growth. Specifically, in this study, we estimated models in which real per capita GDP is explained by remittances and their squared term, controlling for potential growth determinants, such as investment, economic openness, and education. For the empirical analysis, we used unbalanced panel data for 130 developing countries between 1995 and 2013, and applied panel cointegration tests, DOLS, and FMOLS. This study is the first to examine the remittances–growth relationship in developing countries employing these methods.

Our empirical results obtained using FMOLS and DOLS indicate that remittances and their squared term have significantly positive and negative coefficients, respectively. These findings suggest that the relationship between remittances and growth becomes inverted U-shaped and that the effect of remittances on economic growth might change from positive to negative over time. This nonlinear pattern plausibly explains every effect of remittances on economic growth found in empirical studies cited above — that is, positive and negative effects.

Moreover, with regard to the control variables, the investment ratio, economic openness, and school enrollment ratio are found to have significant positive effects on real per capita GDP. In line with many previous studies, these findings indicate that economic growth is accelerated by capital accumulation, trade expansion, and raised education standards.

References

Abida, Z., Sghaier, I. M., 2014. Remittances, financial development and economic growth: The case of North African countries. *The Romanian Economic Journal* 17, 137–170.

Acosta, P., Calderón, C., Fajnzylber, P., López, J. H., 2008. Do remittances lower poverty levels in Latin America? in: Fajnzylber, P., López, J. H. (Eds.), *Remittances and Development: Lessons from Latin America*. World Bank, Washington D.C., pp. 87–132.

Adams, S., Klobodu, E. K. M., 2016. Remittances, regime durability and economic growth in sub-Saharan Africa (SSA). *Economic Analysis and Policy* 50, 1–8.

Ahamada, I., Coulibaly, D., 2013. Remittances and growth in sub-Saharan African countries: Evidence from a panel causality test. *Journal of International Development* 25, 310–324.

Amuedo-Dorantes, C., Pozo, S., 2004. Workers' remittances and the real exchange rate: A paradox of gifts. *World Development* 32, 1407–1417.

Barajas, A., Chami, R., Fullenkamp, C., Gapen, M., Montiel, P., 2009. Do workers' remittances promote economic growth? IMF Working Paper WP/09/153, International Monetary Fund, Washington D.C.

Barro, R. J., 2013. Education and economic growth. *Annals of Economics and Finance* 14, 301–328.

Bettin, G., Zazzaro, A., 2012. Remittances and financial development: Substitutes or complements in economic growth. *Bulletin of Economic Research* 64, 509–536.

Calderón, C., Fajnzylber, P., López, J. H., 2008. Remittances and growth: The role of complementary policies, in: Fajnzylber, P., López, J. H. (Eds.), *Remittances and Development: Lessons from Latin America*. World Bank, Washington D.C., pp. 335–368.

Catrinescu, N., Leon-Ledesma, M., Piracha, M., Quillin, B., 2009. Remittances, institutions, and economic growth. *World Development* 37, 81–92.

Chami, R., Fullenkamp, C., Jahjah, S., 2005. Are immigrant remittance flows a source of capital for development? *IMF Staff Papers* 52, 55–81.

Chowdhury, M., 2016. Financial development, remittances and economic growth: Evidence using a dynamic panel estimation. *Margin — The Journal of Applied Economic Research* 10, 35–54.

Cooray, A., 2012. The impact of migrant remittances on economic growth: Evidence from South Asia. *Review of International Economics* 20, 985–998.

De Long, J. B., Summers, L., 1991. Equipment investment and economic growth. *The Quarterly Journal of Economics* 106, 445–502.

De Long, J. B., Summers, L., 1993. How strongly do developing economies benefit from equipment investment? *Journal of Monetary Economics* 32, 395–415.

Dollar, D., 1992. Outward-oriented developing economies really do grow more rapidly: Evidence from 95 LDCs, 1976–1985. *Economic Development and Cultural Change* 40, 523–544.

Dollar, D., Kraay, A., 2004. Trade, growth, and poverty. *The Economic Journal* 114, F22–F49.

Edwards, S., 1998. Openness, productivity and growth: What do we really know? *The Economic Journal* 108, 383–398.

Fayissa, B., Nsiah, C., 2010. The impact of remittances on economic growth and development in Africa. *The American Economist* 55, 92–103.

Frankel, J. A., Romer, D., 1999. Does trade cause growth? *American Economic Review* 89, 379–399.

Giuliano, P., Ruiz-Arranz, M., 2009. Remittances, financial development, and growth. *Journal of Development Economics* 90, 144–152.

Goschin, Z., 2014. Remittances as an economic development factor: Empirical evidence from the CEE countries. *Procedia Economics and Finance* 10, 54–60.

Imai, K. S., Gaiha, R., Ali, A., Kaicker, N., 2014. Remittances, growth and poverty: New evidence from Asian countries. *Journal of Policy Modeling* 36, 524–538.

International Monetary Fund (IMF), 2005. *World Economic Outlook April 2005: Globalization and External Imbalances.* IMF, Washington D.C.

Johansen, S., 1988. Statistical analysis of cointegration vectors. *Journal of Economic Dynamics and Control* 12, 231–254.

Johansen, S., Juselius, K., 1990. Maximum likelihood estimation and inference on cointegration — With applications to the demand for money. *Oxford Bulletin of Economics and Statistics* 52, 169–209.

Jongwanich, J., 2007. Workers' remittances, economic growth and poverty in developing Asia and the Pacific countries. UNESCAP Working Paper WP/07/01, United Nations Economic and Social Commission for Asia and the Pacific, Bangkok.

Koyame-Marsh, R. O., 2012. The impact of workers' remittances on economic growth: Evidence from ECOWAS countries. *Journal of Third World Studies* 29, 111–130.

Krueger, A. B., Lindahl, M., 2001. Education for growth: Why and for whom? *Journal of Economic Literature* 39, 1101–1136.

Kumar, R. R., 2013. Remittances and economic growth: A study of Guyana. *Economic System* 37, 462–472.

Lartey, E. K. K., 2013. Remittances, investment and growth in sub-Saharan Africa. *The Journal of International Trade & Economic Development* 22, 1038–1058.

Levine, R., Renelt, D., 1992. A sensitivity analysis of cross-country growth regressions. *American Economic Review* 82, 942–963.

Lim, S., Simmons, W. O., 2015. Do remittances promote economic growth in the Caribbean Community and Common Market? *Journal of Economics and Business* 77, 42–59.

Maddala, G. S., Wu, S., 1999. A comparative study of unit root tests with panel data and a new simple test. *Oxford Bulletin of Economics and Statistics* 61, 631–652.

Mankiw, N. G., Romer, D., Weil, D. N., 1992. A contribution to the empirics of economic growth. *The Quarterly Journal of Economics* 107, 407–437.

Meyer, D., Shera, A., 2017. The impact of remittances on economic growth: An econometric model. *EconomiA* 18, 147–155.

Mundaca, B. G., 2009. Remittances, financial market development, and economic growth: The case of Latin America and the Caribbean. *Review of Development Economics* 13, 288–303.

Nsiah, C., Fayissa, B., 2013. Remittances and economic growth in Africa, Asia, and Latin American–Caribbean countries: A panel unit root and panel cointegration analysis. *Journal of Economics and Finance* 37, 424–441.

Nyamongo, E. M., Misati, R. N., Kipyegon, L., Ndirangu, L., 2012. Remittances, financial development and economic growth in Africa. *Journal of Economics and Business* 64, 240–260.

Phillips, P. C. B., Hansen, B. E., 1990. Statistical inference in instrumental variables regression with I(1) processes. *Review of Economic Studies* 57, 99–125.

Pradhan, G., Upadhyay, M., Upadhyaya, K., 2008. Remittances and economic growth in developing countries. *The European Journal of Development Research* 20, 497–506.

Ramirez, M. D., 2013. Do financial and institutional variables enhance the impact of remittances on economic growth in Latin America and the Caribbean? A panel cointegration analysis. *International Advances in Economic Research* 19, 273–288.

Ramirez, M. D., Sharma, H., 2009. Remittances and growth in Latin America: A panel unit root and panel cointegration analysis. *Economic Studies of International Development* 9, 5–36.

Rao, B. B., Hassan, G. M., 2011. A panel data analysis of the growth effects of remittances. *Economic Modelling* 28, 701–709.

Sachs, J. D., Warner, A., 1995. Economic reform and the process of global integration. *Brookings Papers on Economic Activity* 26, 1–118.

Saikkonen, P., 1992. Estimation and testing of cointegrated systems by an autoregressive approximation. *Econometric Theory* 8, 1–27.

Senbeta, A., 2013. Remittances and the sources of growth. *Applied Economics Letters* 20, 572–580.

Singh, R. J., Haacker, M., Lee, K-W., Goff, M. L., 2011. Determinants and macroeconomic impact of remittances in sub-Saharan Africa. *Journal of African Economies* 20, 312–340.

Stock, J. H., Watson, M. W., 1993. A simple estimator of cointegrating vectors in higher order integrated systems. *Econometrica* 61, 783–820.

Vargas-Silva, C., Jha, S., Sugiyarto, G., 2009. Remittances in Asia: Implications for the fight against poverty and the pursuit of economic growth. ADB Economic Working Paper Series 182, Asian Development Bank, Manila.

World Bank, 2014. *World Development Indicators*. World Bank, Washington D.C., http://databank.worldbank.org/data/source/world-development-indicators, Accessed 5 November 2014.

Chapter 4

Remittance Inflows and Poverty Reduction: How Economic Development Affects Remittances' Effect on Poverty Reduction

4.1 Introduction

Since the 2000s, international remittance flows have increased significantly, becoming the most important external source of finance for developing countries after foreign direct investment (FDI). Against the background of a surge in these capital inflows, a growing body of literature has empirically investigated the effects of remittances on the well-being of residents in recipient countries. The relevant studies have generally revealed that remittances have a poverty-reducing effect in developing countries. However, just as poverty is not distributed equally across developing countries, migrants' remittances are not distributed equally across regions.

In Figure 4.1, we separate the developing world into six geographical regions and compare the amounts of remittances received by these regions.[1] This figure shows that remittances have risen significantly in South Asia and East Asia and the Pacific (EAP), especially since the year 2000, followed by Latin America and the Caribbean (LAC), the Middle East and North Africa (MENA), Europe and Central Asia, and sub-Saharan Africa. Since the year 2000, five of the world's top 10 remittance-receiving countries have been in

---

[1]We use a geographical criterion set by the World Bank.

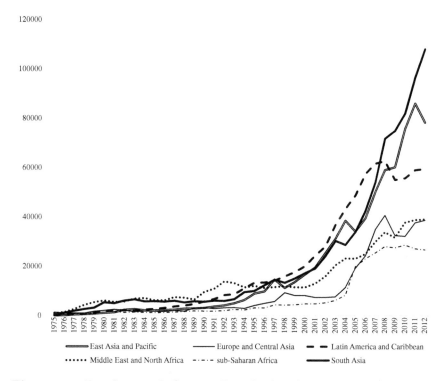

Figure 4.1   Remittance Inflows to Developing Countries by Geographical Region (US\$ million)

Source: World Bank (2014).

Asia (India, China, the Philippines, Pakistan, and Bangladesh), accounting for approximately 37% of the total remittance inflows to developing countries. This trend is considered to reflect the consistently increasing net migration rate in South Asia and EAP since the early 1990s and late 1990s, respectively.

In Figure 4.2, we separate the developing world into three groups based on the income criterion and compare the amounts of remittances received by these groups.[2] From this figure, we find that remittances have increased significantly in lower middle-income countries, especially since the early 2000s, followed by upper

---

[2]We use an income criterion set by the World Bank.

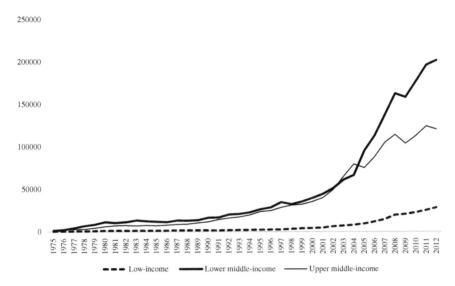

Figure 4.2 Remittance Inflows to Developing Countries by Income Group (US$ million)
Source: World Bank (2014).

middle-income countries. On the other hand, remittance inflows show a slight increase in low-income countries. People migrate to other countries for several reasons. Economically speaking, unemployment or low income in the home country drives people to work abroad. Conversely, very low-income households find it difficult to afford the costs of international migration. Therefore, more people supposedly migrate and send money home from lower middle-income countries than from other income group countries.

So far, several studies have considered the geographical trend of remittances in order to analyze the poverty-reducing effect of remittances. For example, Adams and Page (2005) and Acosta *et al.* (2008) include regional dummies in estimating the effects of migration and/or remittances on poverty conditions. Similarly, Vargas-Silva *et al.* (2009), Anyanwu and Erhijakpor (2010), and Gaaliche and Zayati (2015) analyze the poverty-reducing effect of remittances by limiting their samples to Asia, Africa, and Central and Eastern Europe and the MENA, respectively. However, no relevant study explicitly considers the different stages of economic development measured by per capita income level. We aim to fill this gap in the literature by examining whether the effect of remittances on poverty changes over the course of economic development.

Specifically, we consider remittances, per capita income, and their interaction term as the principal explanatory variables. Then, we estimate models in which the poverty headcount ratio is explained by these variables and several other control variables. We apply the generalized method of moments (GMM) to panel data from 120 developing countries during 1975–2013. Given that a lower poverty ratio means an improvement of poverty conditions, if the coefficients of remittances, per capita income, and their interaction term have negative signs, this would suggest that there is a larger poverty-reducing effect of remittances in developing countries with higher income than in developing countries with lower income. This implies that, as the recipient country develops economically, remittances will become a more powerful instrument for poverty reduction in this country. On the other hand, if the coefficients of remittances and per capita income have negative signs, but the coefficient of their interaction term has a positive sign, this finding implies that the poverty-reducing effect of remittances tends to be lower in developing countries with higher income. In other words, remittances contribute not only to the reduction of extreme global poverty but also to the reduction of income inequality across developing countries, since the poverty-reducing effect of remittances becomes larger in recipient countries with lower income.

The structure of the rest of this chapter is as follows. Section 4.2 briefly reviews the relevant literature. Section 4.3 presents the model. Section 4.4 provides the definitions, sources, and properties of the data. Section 4.5 provides the empirical results. Finally, Section 4.6 summarizes our main findings.

4.2   Literature Review

Remittance inflows are thought to reduce poverty in recipient countries through several channels. For example, remittances might help remitters' family members in their home countries to obtain additional income and thereby enable them to smooth and expand their consumption, which ameliorates poverty conditions (the International Monetary Fund (IMF), 2005, pp. 72–73). In addition, remittances can be used to improve the health and education of recipient households, which contributes to improving the living standards of especially poor families (*ibid.*, pp. 72–73).

Against the background of a surge in remittance inflows to developing countries, a growing body of literature has empirically analyzed the effect of remittances on poverty reduction in developing countries. Table 4.1 summarizes the related empirical studies on the effect of remittances on poverty conditions. These studies can be categorized broadly into two groups.

The first group aims to explore the direct effect of remittances on poverty conditions, including such studies as Adams and Page (2005), the IMF (2005), Jongwanich (2007), Gupta *et al.* (2009), Vargas-Silva *et al.* (2009), Anyanwu and Erhijakpor (2010), Serino and Kim (2011), the United Nations (2011), Imai *et al.* (2014), Gaaliche and Zayati (2015), and Azam *et al.* (2016). These studies empirically investigate whether and how remittances affect poverty across countries using the poverty ratio, poverty gap, and/or squared poverty gap as measures of poverty conditions.

For example, Adams and Page (2005) examine the effect of remittances on poverty using data for 71 developing countries. Poverty is measured using three indicators: poverty headcount ratio, poverty gap, and squared poverty gap. They define international remittances as either the share of migrants in a country's population or the per capita international remittances received by residents of a developing country. Using the ordinary least squares (OLS) and instrumental variable estimations, the authors show that international remittances have a negative and statistically significant effect on all poverty indicators, whereas the share of migrants has a negative and statistically significant effect on all poverty indicators except the squared poverty gap.

Gupta *et al.* (2009) investigate the effect of remittances on poverty for 76 developing countries from 1980 to 2003. The authors estimate a system of equations in which both poverty and remittances are endogenously determined by the three-stage least squares (3SLS)

Table 4.1 Summary of Literature on the Remittances — Poverty Nexus

Author(s)	Countries Period	Variables	Method(s)	Results
Adams and Page (2005)	71 developing countries 1983–1999	*Dependent variable:* poverty headcount ratio, poverty gap, or squared poverty gap *Independent variables:* per capita official international remittances or share of migrants in a country's population, real per capita GDP or per capita survey mean income, Gini coefficient, regional dummies All variables are transformed into logarithms.	OLS or IV, Panel	Remittances have a negative and significant effect on all three of the poverty measures. For example, after instrumenting for possible endogeneity, a 10% increase in per capita official international remittances will lead to a 3.5% decline in the poverty ratio, a 4.0% decline in the poverty gap, and a 2.8% decline in the squared poverty gap.
IMF (2005)	90 countries 1970–2003	*Dependent variable:* poverty headcount ratio or poverty gap *Independent variables:* remittances to GDP ratio, average income, Gini coefficient All variables are transformed into logarithms.	IV, Cross-country	There is a strong link between poverty and remittances. The effect may seem to be economically small. However, the analysis controls separately for the effect of average income

(*Continued*)

Table 4.1 (*Continued*)

Author(s)	Countries Period	Variables	Method(s)	Results
				and income inequality, and these variables are themselves likely to be influenced by remittances. As a result, the true effect of remittances on poverty may be substantially larger.
Jongwanich (2007)	17 countries in Asia and the Pacific 1993–2003 (3-year average)	*Dependent variable:* poverty headcount ratio *Independent variables:* remittances as a share of GDP, growth of real per capita GDP, human development index, inflation rate, goods exports and goods imports to total output ratio, Gini coefficient All variables are transformed into logarithms.	Fixed effects-IV, Panel	Remittances have a significant direct effect on poverty reduction through increasing income, smoothing consumption, and easing capital constraints of poor people.

(*Continued*)

Table 4.1 (*Continued*)

Author(s)	Countries Period	Variables	Method(s)	Results
Acosta *et al.* (2008)	N/A	*Dependent variable:* (1) the log difference of per capita income (2) the log difference of Gini coefficient *Independent variables:* (1) remittances (the log of lagged remittances as a percentage of GDP), the interaction term between remittances and regional dummy for Latin America, the log of lagged per capita income, average years of secondary education of the female and male population, the price of investment goods (2) remittances, the interaction term between remittances and regional dummy for Latin America, the log of the lagged Gini coefficient, average years of secondary education of the female and male population, the price of investment goods	System GMM, Panel	(1) Remittances tend to be good for economic growth both at the global level and in Latin America. (2) Remittances seem to lead to higher income inequality at the global level, but either reduce inequality or leave it unchanged in Latin America. Therefore, remittances tend to reduce poverty in Latin America.

(*Continued*)

Table 4.1   (*Continued*)

Author(s)	Countries Period	Variables	Method(s)	Results
Gupta *et al.* (2009)	76 countries N/A	*Dependent variable:* poverty headcount ratio, poverty gap, or squared poverty gap *Independent variables:* remittances to GDP ratio, real per capita GDP, Gini coefficient All variables are transformed into logarithms. All independent variables are averages for 5-year periods.	OLS or 3SLS, Panel	Remittances have a negative effect on poverty indexes. Except in the case in which the dependent variable is the squared poverty gap, this effect is statistically significant at the 5% level. However, the results from the 3SLS indicate that the average remittance-inducing elasticity of poverty is consistently greater than the average poverty-reducing elasticity of remittances.

(*Continued*)

Table 4.1 (*Continued*)

Author(s)	Countries Period	Variables	Method(s)	Results
Portes (2009)	46 countries 1970–2000	*Dependent variable:* the log of decile income *Independent variables:* the log of real remittances, the log of the interaction term between real remittances and low-income country dummy variable, the log of per capita GDP, secondary school enrollment ratio, inflation rate, exports and imports to GDP ratio	Pooled OLS, Panel	The effect of remittances on decile income is larger in low-income countries than in the whole sample. The effect of remittances on mean income is positive and decreasing in income for the bottom 70% of the population, and negative and increasing in income in the top 20% of the population. Therefore, remittances not only reduce poverty, but also reduce income inequality.

(*Continued*)

Table 4.1 (*Continued*)

Author(s)	Countries Period	Variables	Method(s)	Results
Vargas-Silva *et al.* (2009)	20 countries in Asia 1988–2007	*Dependent variable:* poverty headcount ratio or poverty gap *Independent variables:* remittances as a percentage of GDP, per capita GDP, gross capital formation as a percentage of GDP, exports and imports as a percentage of GDP, inflation rate All variables except for inflation rate are transformed into natural logarithms.	Fixed effects or Random effects, Panel	Remittances have a negligible effect on the poverty ratio, but they tend to decrease the poverty gap. The estimates suggest that a 10% increase in remittances decreases the poverty gap by about 0.7–1.4%. Therefore, remittances ameliorate the depth of poverty.
Anyanwu and Erhijakpor (2010)	33 countries in Africa 1990–2005	*Dependent variable:* poverty headcount ratio, poverty gap, or squared poverty gap *Independent variables:* remittances as a percentage of GDP, Gini coefficient, real per capita GDP, adult literacy rate, inflation rate, exports and imports to GDP ratio, sub-Saharan Africa regional dummy All variables are transformed into logarithms.	OLS or IV-GMM, Panel	Remittances have a negative and significant effect on all three measures of poverty in Africa. After instrumenting for the possible endogeneity of remittances, a 10% increase in remittances leads to a 2.9% decline in the poverty headcount ratio and the poverty gap, and a 2.8% decline in the squared poverty gap, respectively.

(Continued)

Table 4.1 (*Continued*)

Author(s)	Countries Period	Variables	Method(s)	Results
Serino and Kim (2011)	66 developing countries 1981–2005	*Dependent variable:* poverty headcount ratio, poverty gap, or squared poverty gap *Independent variables:* remittances to GDP ratio, real per capita GDP, Gini coefficient, FDI to GDP ratio, ODA to GDP ratio All independent variables are transformed into logarithms.	OLS or Quantile regression, Panel	Remittances have uneven effects across poverty quantiles for developing countries. The poverty-alleviating effect of remittances is more pronounced in the worst-off group.
United Nations (2011)	(1) 77 developing countries (2) 29 developing countries with remittances to GDP ratio higher than 5%	*Dependent variable:* poverty headcount ratio or poverty gap *Independent variables:* remittances to GDP ratio, real per capita GDP, Gini coefficient All variables are transformed into logarithms.	3SLS, Panel	(1) Remittances have a significant negative effect on the poverty headcount ratio, but the effect on the poverty gap is not statistically significant. (2)(3) Remittances have a significant effect on both the poverty headcount

(*Continued*)

Table 4.1 (*Continued*)

Author(s)	Countries Period	Variables	Method(s)	Results
	(3) 21 developing countries in Asia with remittances to GDP ratio higher than 5%			ratio and the poverty gap. The positive effect is stronger in Asian developing countries than all developing countries with 5% or more share of remittances in GDP.
	1980–2008			
Imai *et al.* (2014)	24 countries in Asia and the Pacific 1980–2009	*Dependent variable:* poverty headcount ratio *Independent variables:* remittances, growth of real per capita GDP, gross capital formation, financial deepening (deposit money bank assets as a share of deposit money and central bank assets), exports and imports All variables are transformed into logarithms. All independent variables except for growth of real per capita GDP and financial deepening are expressed as a percentage of GDP	Fixed effects 2SLS, Panel	Remittances contribute to poverty reduction through their direct effects. For example, in the case of the poverty headcount ratio (US$ 1.25), the direct effect is much larger than the indirect effect in absolute terms and the total effect of remittances on poverty is −0.128, implying that a 1% increase in the share of remittances leads to a 0.128% decrease in the poverty ratio, *ceteris paribus*.

(*Continued*)

Table 4.1 *(Continued)*

Author(s)	Countries Period	Variables	Method(s)	Results
Gaaliche and Zayati (2015)	14 emerging and developing countries in Central and Eastern Europe and the MENA 1980–2012	(1) *Dependent variable:* poverty headcount ratio *Independent variables:* remittances to GDP ratio, real per capita GDP, Gini coefficient (2) poverty headcount ratio, remittances to GDP ratio All variables are transformed into logarithms.	(1) FMOLS, Panel (2) Granger causality test, Panel	(1) Remittances have a role in reducing poverty in the recipient countries, although the effect is relatively small. (2) The relationship between remittances and the poverty ratio is bidirectional. The causal effect of poverty reduction on remittances is stronger than the reverse effect is.
Azam *et al.* (2016)	Nine high-income countries, 15 upper middle-income countries, 13 lower middle-income countries 1990–2014	*Dependent variable:* poverty headcount ratio *Independent variables:* remittances, per capita GDP, inflation rate, secondary school enrollment ratio, net ODA All variables are transformed into logarithms.	FMOLS, Panel	Remittances have a positive effect on poverty reduction, but the effect is statistically insignificant in lower middle-income and high-income countries. In upper middle-income countries, a 1% increase in remittances decreases the poverty ratio by 0.201%.

method. Their results indicate a poverty-reducing effect of remittances, similar in magnitude to the effect they estimate through OLS. However, the average poverty-reducing elasticity of remittances is consistently found to be smaller than the average remittance-inducing elasticity of poverty. Therefore, the authors indicate the possibility that the effect of poverty on out-migration and remittance inflows might be greater than the effect of remittances on poverty reduction.

Imai *et al.* (2014) analyze whether remittances alleviate poverty in 24 Asian and Pacific countries from 1980 to 2009. The authors use a poverty ratio based on US\$ 1.25 or US\$ 2.00 a day at 2005 international prices as their measure of poverty and apply fixed-effects two-stage least squares (2SLS) estimation. The results of Imai *et al.* (2014) show that remittances reduce poverty in Asia-Pacific developing countries, especially through their direct effects. For example, in the case of the US\$ 1.25 poverty line, the magnitude of the effect of remittances on poverty indicates that a 1% increase in the share of remittances in GDP leads to a 0.128% decrease in the poverty ratio, *ceteris paribus.*

The second group of studies indirectly examines how remittances influence poverty conditions in remittance-receiving countries through income level and income distribution.[3] For example, Acosta *et al.* (2008) specify a model in which the dependent variables are the changes in per capita GDP and the Gini coefficient, and the main independent variables are remittances and the interaction term between remittances and the LAC regional dummy. Using panel data of 59 developing countries, Acosta *et al.* (2008) find that remittances have a positive effect on average income in the LAC region, but that they have a negative or negligible effect on income inequality in the

---

[3]Koechlin and Leon (2007) analyze what kind of relationship might exist between remittances and income inequality. At the first stage of migration history, migration is assumed to be limited to high-income households that can afford high migration costs. As more people migrate and the cost of migration decreases, however, migration becomes more accessible for low-income households, which leads to an income-equalizing effect. Using cross-country data for 78 countries, Koechlin and Leon (2007) find an inverted U-shaped relationship between remittances and income inequality.

same region. Therefore, the authors conclude that remittances reduce poverty in LAC.

Similarly, Portes (2009) explores the effect of remittances across the distribution of income. Using a panel of 46 countries during 1970–2000, the author estimates models in which average income of each decile is determined by remittances, per capita GDP, and several other control variables. Portes (2009) finds that the effect of remittances is positive and decreasing in income for the bottom 70% of the population and negative and increasing in income for the top 20% of the population, concluding that remittances contribute to reducing not only income inequality but also poverty. Therefore, the second group of studies also confirms the poverty-reducing effect of remittances through income level and income distribution.

4.3 Model

As shown in Section 4.2, the literature indicates that remittance inflows have a significant effect on poverty reduction in developing countries. In this study, we investigate the extent to which the poverty-reducing effect of remittances is affected by the stage of economic development of remittance-receiving countries. Specifically, we examine whether and how remittances contribute to poverty reduction by considering differences in income levels of developing countries. As with the first group of studies mentioned in Section 4.2, this study investigates the direct effect of remittances on poverty conditions using the poverty ratio as the dependent variable. With reference to the second group of studies, we also analyze how the effect of remittances on poverty conditions changes depending on the income level of the recipient country. In this sense, the present study combines the characteristics of the first and second groups of the relevant literature.

We use the following dynamic panel model for the empirical analysis:

$$POV_{i,t} = \alpha + \gamma POV_{i,t-1} + \beta_1 REM_{i,t} + \beta_2 GDP_{i,t}$$
$$+ \beta_3 OPEN_{i,t} + \beta_4 INF_{i,t} + \beta_5 REM_{i,t} \times GDP_{i,t} + u_{i,t},$$
$$u_{i,t} = \nu_i + \varepsilon_{i,t}, \qquad i = 1, 2, \ldots, N, t = 1, 2, \ldots, T, \qquad (4.1)$$

where ν_i is the individual effects, and the error term $(\varepsilon_{i,t})$ satisfies the following properties:

$$E(\varepsilon_{i,t}) = 0, \quad E(\varepsilon_{i,s}\varepsilon_{i,t}) = \begin{cases} \sigma_\varepsilon^2 \ (s = t) \\ 0 \ (s \neq t) \end{cases}.$$

The explained variable in Equation (4.1) is the poverty headcount ratio (POV). This study focuses on the effect of remittances (REM) on the poverty ratio. We control some variables, such as the log of real per capita GDP (GDP), the ratio of exports and imports of goods and services to GDP $(OPEN)$, and the inflation rate (INF). In addition, we consider the effect of the interaction term between remittances and real per capita GDP in logarithms $(REM \times GDP)$ in our analysis.

According to Equation (4.1), the partial derivative of the poverty ratio with respect to remittances can be expressed as

$$\frac{\partial POV_{i,t}}{\partial REM_{i,t}} = \beta_1 + \beta_5 GDP_{i,t}. \tag{4.2}$$

Equation (4.2) indicates that the effects of remittances on the poverty ratio depend on the level of per capita GDP. If the sign of β_5 differs from that of β_1, the effect of remittances on the poverty ratio will be offset as real per capita GDP increases.

4.4 Data

We prepare a panel dataset of 183 non-Organisation for Economic Co-operation and Development countries over the period 1970–2013. The variables, such as remittances and per capita income, are not expected to have immediate effects on poverty reduction. Therefore, we construct data for every five years from 1970 to 2009 and take a four-year average from 2010 to 2013. Since there are no poverty ratio data for 1970, we start the sample from 1975, and thus the sample size over the time series is eight years.[4] In addition, because there are no poverty data for 63 countries, there are 120 countries used in the analysis.

---

[4]The time series is the following: 1975–1979, 1980–1984, 1985–1989, 1990–1994, 1995–1999, 2000–2004, 2005–2009, and 2010–2013.

The poverty ratio (*POV*) is used as the dependent variable in this empirical analysis. This study measures the poverty ratio by the poverty headcount ratio at US$ 1.25 a day (measured as a percentage of the population). The poverty data are obtained from the World Development Indicators published by the World Bank (2014).

Remittances (*REM*) represent the important explanatory variable on which we focus in this study. Remittances are personal remittances received and are defined as the percentage of GDP. The remittances data are obtained from the World Bank (2014). Figure 4.3 illustrates the movements of the ratio of personal remittances to GDP over the period 1975–2013. As is clear from this figure, the remittance ratio is likely to increase as time passes. The receipt of remittances is expected to raise the incomes of migrants' family members in their home countries for consumption, investment, and savings, and thereby improve their standards of living. Therefore, the coefficient of *REM* in Equation (4.1) is expected to be negative.

The log of real per capita GDP (*GDP*) is the per capita GDP in logarithms (constant 2005 US$). These GDP data are obtained from the World Bank (2014). Roemer and Gugerty (1997) find that the relationship between the income of poor people and average income is exactly one-to-one when poor people are defined as the

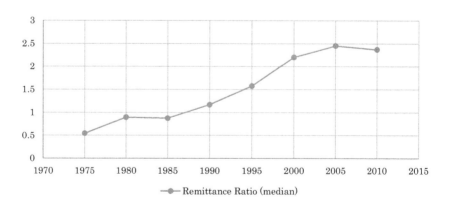

Figure 4.3   Remittance Ratio (Median)

Note: Personal remittances, received, as a percentage of GDP.
Source: World Bank (2014).

bottom 40% of the income distribution. Since economic growth, as measured by increases in average income per capita, is considered an effective instrument for poverty reduction, the coefficient of GDP in Equation (4.1) is expected to be negative.

Some relevant literatures indicate that the other variables do not have an independent effect on the income of poor people once the income effect has been considered (Roemer and Gugerty, 1997). On the other hand, other studies suggest that certain policies can have direct effects on the income of poor people even after controlling for the effect of economic growth (Collier and Dollar, 2001; Ghura *et al.*, 2002). Therefore, we add other factors influencing poverty as control variables, namely, economic openness and the inflation rate.

Economic openness ($OPEN$) is measured by the ratio of exports and imports to GDP. These data are obtained from the World Bank (2014). The effect of economic openness on poverty conditions is ambiguous. On the one hand, if trade liberalization worsens income distribution, it is possible that liberalization is not good for poverty reduction, despite its positive overall growth effects (Anyanwu and Erhijakpor, 2010). Indeed, Milanovic (2005, p. 31) finds that "openness seems to have a particularly negative effect on poor and middle-income groups in poor countries." Moreover, Hamori and Hashiguchi (2012) suggest that, in poor countries, globalization benefits only those with basic and high education and lowers the income share of those with no education. By contrast, several other studies using cross-sectional and panel datasets indicate that economic openness reduces poverty (Bergh and Nilsson, 2014) and benefits poor people at least as much as the average person through economic growth (Dollar and Kraay, 2004). Since empirical studies have provided inconclusive evidence, we cannot *a priori* predict the sign of the economic openness coefficient in Equation (4.1).

As a control variable, we also measure the inflation rate (INF) as the annual percentage of consumer prices. These data are obtained from the World Bank (2014). Easterly and Fischer (2001) find that high inflation tends to lower the share of the bottom quintile and the real minimum wage, while it tends to increase poverty in various cross-country and cross-time samples. Other studies confirm the negative effects of inflation on the well-being of poor people and poverty reduction (Romer and Romer, 1998; Akhter and Liu, 2010; Jeanneney and Kpodar, 2011). In line with these studies, we expect the coefficient of INF to have a positive sign in Equation (4.1).

Furthermore, our empirical specification includes the interaction term between remittances and the log of real per capita GDP as an explanatory variable. This term indicates how the effects of remittances on the poverty ratio change as the level of GDP increases.

The definitions and sources of the data for each variable are given in Table 4.2. Table 4.3 presents summary statistics for each variable.

Table 4.2   Definition and Source of Each Variable

Variable	Definition	Source
POV	Poverty headcount ratio at US$ 1.25 a day as a percentage of the population	World Bank (2014)
REM	Personal remittances, received, as a percentage of GDP	
GDP	Logarithm of real per capita GDP (constant 2005 US$)	
OPEN	Exports and imports of goods and services as a percentage of GDP	
INF	Inflation, consumer prices (%)	

Table 4.3   Summary Statistics

	POV	REM	GDP	OPEN	INF
Mean	23.779	4.389	7.137	75.483	53.357
Standard deviation	24.870	8.553	1.082	38.487	330.650
Skewness	0.906	5.420	−0.001	1.052	12.953
Kurtosis	2.553	43.838	2.002	4.948	210.596
Jarque–Bera	68.896	53,112.260	35.354	285.019	1,376,838.000
p-value (Jarque–Bera)	(0.000)	(0.000)	(0.000)	(0.000)	(0.000)
Number of observations	475	714	852	832	755

4.5 Empirical Results

The estimation results of Equation (4.1) are divided into three cases. They are reported in Table 4.4. The explanatory variables of each case are as follows:

Case 1: $POV_{i,t-1}$, $REM_{i,t}$, and $GDP_{i,t}$,

Case 2: $POV_{i,t-1}$, $REM_{i,t}$, $GDP_{i,t}$, $OPEN_{i,t}$, and $INF_{i,t}$,

Case 3: $POV_{i,t-1}$, $REM_{i,t}$, $GDP_{i,t}$, $OPEN_{i,t}$, $INF_{i,t}$,
    and $REM_{i,t} \times GDP_{i,t}$.

Along with the estimated coefficients for the explanatory variables, Table 4.4 shows their standard errors and p-values.

For the empirical results shown in Table 4.4, the estimations of the coefficients in Equation (4.1) are as follows. First, the coefficients of remittances are negative as expected and statistically significant at the conventional levels in all cases (-0.743 for Case 1, -0.703 for Case 2, and -9.510 for Case 3). These results indicate that an increase in remittances leads to poverty reduction.

In addition, Table 4.4 shows the estimation results of the control variables, namely, per capita GDP, economic openness, and the inflation rate. The coefficients of per capita GDP in logarithms are estimated to be -17.389 for Case 1, -12.322 for Case 2, and -15.434 for Case 3. The coefficients are statistically significant at the 1% level in all cases. Therefore, these results suggest that a rise of per capita GDP leads to poverty reduction. Next, the coefficients of economic openness are estimated to be negative (-0.044 for Case 2 and -0.028 for Case 3), but they are not statistically significant. Thus, a rise of openness has no significant effect on the poverty ratio. The coefficients of the inflation rate are estimated to be 0.006 for Cases 2 and 3, and both coefficients are statistically significant. Therefore, an increased inflation rate might increase the poverty ratio.

Finally, the coefficient of the interaction term between remittances and real per capita GDP is estimated to be 1.225 and statistically significant at the conventional level. We find that remittances have a negative effect on the poverty ratio. In addition, we find that the interaction term between remittances and real per capita GDP

Table 4.4 Empirical Results

Variable	Case 1			Case 2			Case 3		
	Estimate	SE	p-value	Estimate	SE	p-value	Estimate	SE	p-value
POV (−1)	0.328	0.071	0.000	0.399	0.074	0.000	0.356	0.076	0.000
REM	−0.743	0.235	0.002	−0.703	0.250	0.006	−9.510	5.218	0.071
GDP	−17.389	1.300	0.000	−12.322	2.506	0.000	−15.434	2.643	0.000
OPEN				−0.044	0.050	0.382	−0.028	0.052	0.593
INF				0.006	0.002	0.000	0.006	0.002	0.000
REM × GDP							1.225	0.722	0.092
J-statistic	24.578			19.226			18.540		
p-value (J-statistic)	(0.137)			(0.507)			(0.487)		

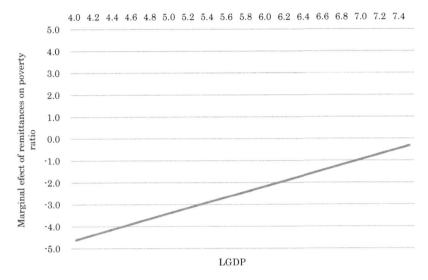

Figure 4.4 Marginal Effects of Remittances on Poverty Ratio Conditional on Real Per Capita GDP

Note: The marginal effect is indicated as $\frac{\partial POV_{i,t}}{\partial REM_{i,t}} = \beta_1 + \beta_5 GDP_{i,t}$.

has a statically significant positive effect, which indicates that the negative effects of remittances on the poverty ratio are mitigated as a country becomes richer. The marginal effect of remittances on the poverty ratio is plotted in Figure 4.4. In this figure, the horizontal axis indicates the logarithm of per capita GDP and the vertical axis indicates the marginal effect of the change in remittances on the poverty ratio. As is clear from this figure, the marginal effect is negative from the minimum to the maximum levels of per capita income.

In summary, Table 4.4 shows that remittances have a positive effect on poverty reduction, but this effect changes depending on real per capita GDP. As a country becomes richer, the effect of remittances on the country's poverty ratio becomes smaller, although remittances still have a poverty-reducing effect. With regard to the control variables, an increase in real per capita GDP leads to a decrease in the poverty ratio, whereas an increase in the inflation rate leads to an increase of the poverty ratio.

4.6   Concluding Remarks

Extant empirical literature finds that remittance inflows have a significant salutary effect on poverty reduction in developing countries (Adams and Page, 2005; IMF, 2005; Jongwanich, 2007; Acosta *et al.*, 2008; Gupta *et al.*, 2009; Portes, 2009; Vargas-Silva *et al.*, 2009; Anyanwu and Erhijakpor, 2010; Serino and Kim, 2011; United Nations, 2011; Imai *et al.*, 2014; Gaaliche and Zayati, 2015; Azam *et al.*, 2016). Some of these studies also analyze the differences in the poverty-reducing effect of remittances among geographical regions. Unlike these studies, we examine whether and how the poverty-reducing effect of remittances is affected by the income levels of recipient countries. Specifically, we consider remittances, per capita income, and their interaction term as the principal explanatory variables. Then, we estimate models in which the poverty headcount ratio is explained by these variables and several other control variables. We apply the GMM to panel data from 120 developing countries during 1975–2013. The main findings of our study are as follows.

First, remittances and per capita income have the effect of reducing the poverty headcount ratio. Globally, poverty has been improving for the last few decades. The percentage of the population in developing countries living on less than US$ 1.25 per day declined from 56% in 1981 to 18% in 2011. Our findings empirically confirm that expanding inflows of remittances as well as economic growth contribute to poverty alleviation in developing countries. These results are consistent with those of the relevant empirical literature.

Second, the poverty-reducing effect of remittances declines as per capita income increases in the recipient countries, although the effect of remittances on poverty reduction remains positive. In other words, the poverty-reducing effect of remittances would be larger in lower-income countries. Accordingly, remittance inflows are expected to reduce extreme poverty centered in low-income countries, which in turn leads to narrow income gaps between developing countries.

Migrants' remittances can be regarded as global wealth redistribution through private income transfers, which provides benefits to both the host and home countries: the host countries could employ migrants to compensate for labor shortages, while remittances have more positive effects on the well-being of people in poorer remittance-receiving countries. In order to enhance the effect of remittances on poverty conditions, it would be more important for low-income countries to attract more remittances by lowering the fees for money transfer services through formal financial intermediaries, creating a safe and secure environment for online remittances, and providing effective ways to use the money sent by migrants in their home countries.

References

Acosta, P., Calderón, C., Fajnzylber, P., López, J. H., 2008. Do remittances lower poverty levels in Latin America? in: Fajnzylber, P., López, J. H. (Eds.), *Remittances and Development: Lessons from Latin America*. World Bank, Washington D.C., pp. 87–132.

Adams Jr, R. H., Page, J., 2005. Do international migration and remittances reduce poverty in developing countries? *World Development* 33, 1645–1669.

Akhter, S., Liu, Y., 2010. Cross-country evidence on the linkages between financial development and poverty. *International Journal of Business and Management* 5, 3–19.

Anyanwu, J. C., Erhijakpor, A. E. O., 2010. Do international remittances affect poverty in Africa? *African Development Review* 22, 51–91.

Azam, M., Haseeb, M., Samsudin, S., 2016. The impact of foreign remittances on poverty alleviation: Global evidence. *Economics and Sociology* 9, 264–281.

Bergh, A., Nilsson, T., 2014. Is globalization reducing absolute poverty? *World Development* 62, 42–61.

Collier, P., Dollar, D., 2001. Can the world cut poverty in half? How policy reform and effective aid can meet international development goals. *World Development* 29, 1787–1802.

Dollar, D., Kraay, A., 2004. Trade, growth, and poverty. *The Economic Journal* 114, F22–F49.

Easterly, W., Fischer, S., 2001. Inflation and the poor. *Journal of Money, Credit and Banking* 33, 160–178.

Gaaliche, M., Zayati, M., 2015. The causal relationship between remittances and poverty reduction in developing country: Using a non-stationary dynamic panel data. *Journal of Globalization Studies* 6, 30–39.

Ghura, D., Leite, C. A., Tsangarides, C., 2002. Is growth enough? Macroeconomic policy and poverty reduction. IMF Working Paper WP/02/118, International Monetary Fund, Washington D.C.

Gupta, S., Pattillo, C. A., Wagh, S., 2009. Effect of remittances on poverty and financial development in sub-Saharan Africa. *World Development* 37, 104–115.

Hamori, S., Hashiguchi, Y., 2012. The effect of financial deepening on inequality: Some international evidence. *Journal of Asian Economics* 23, 353–359.

Imai, K. S., Gaiha, R., Ali, A., Kaicker, N., 2014. Remittances, growth and poverty: New evidence from Asian countries. *Journal of Policy Modeling* 36, 524–538.

International Monetary Fund (IMF), 2005. *World Economic Outlook April 2005: Globalization and External Imbalances*. IMF, Washington D.C.

Jeanneney, S. G., Kpodar, K., 2011. Financial development and poverty reduction: Can there be a benefit without a cost? *Journal of Development Studies* 47, 143–163.

Jongwanich, J., 2007. Workers' remittances, economic growth and poverty in developing Asia and the Pacific countries. UNESCAP Working Paper WP/07/01, United Nations Economic and Social Commission for Asia and the Pacific, Bangkok.

Koechlin, V., Leon, G., 2007. International remittances and income inequality: An empirical investigation. *Journal of Economic Policy Reform* 10, 123–141.

Milanovic, B., 2005. Can we discern the effect of globalization on income distribution? Evidence from household surveys. *The World Bank Economic Review* 19, 21–44.

Portes, L. S. V., 2009. Remittances, poverty and inequality. *Journal of Economic Development* 34, 127–140.

Roemer, M., Gugerty, M. K., 1997. Does economic growth reduce poverty? CAER II Discussion Paper 4, Harvard Institute for International Development, Cambridge.

Romer, C. D., Romer, D. H., 1998. Monetary policy and the well-being of the poor. NBER Working Paper Series 6793, National Bureau of Economic Research, Cambridge.

Serino, M. N. V., Kim, D., 2011. How do international remittances affect poverty in developing countries? A quantile regression analysis. *Journal of Economic Development* 36, 17–40.

United Nations, 2011. *Impact of Remittances on Poverty in Developing Countries*. United Nations, New York and Geneva.

Vargas-Silva, C., Jha, S., Sugiyarto, G., 2009. Remittances in Asia: Implications for the fight against poverty and the pursuit of economic growth. ADB Economics Working Paper Series 182, Asian Development Bank, Manila.

World Bank, 2014. *World Development Indicators*. World Bank, Washington D.C., http://databank.worldbank.org/data/source/world-development-indicators, Accessed 5 November 2014.

Chapter 5

Remittance Inflows and Financial Inclusion: Do Workers' Remittances Promote Access to Finance?

5.1 Introduction

As finance has become increasingly recognized as a powerful tool to promote economic growth and reduce poverty, a growing body of empirical research has investigated the factors affecting the promotion of financial development. One of the potential leading factors is migrants' remittances. Indeed, most recent studies have revealed that remittances are positively associated with financial deepening (e.g., Martínez Pería et al., 2008; Gupta et al., 2009; Aggarwal et al., 2011; Chowdhury, 2011; Demirgüç-Kunt et al., 2011; Cooray, 2012).[1] This finding suggests that recipient households deposit their surplus money in financial institutions, which in turn increases loanable funds from financial institutions to the private sector.

This study differs from this strand of literature in that it specifically examines financial development in terms of financial inclusion, rather than financial deepening. The fact that remittances increase financial deepening does not necessarily mean that remittances promote financial inclusion (Anzoategui et al., 2014, p. 339). Remittances are expected to contribute to promoting access to

---

[1]Unlike most studies, Brown et al. (2013), using annual panel data for 138 countries from 1970 to 2005, indicate that remittances seem to be negatively associated with domestic credit to the private sector in terms of percentage of GDP, although this negative effect is small.

finance if unbanked recipient households become willing to demand the safe storage of surplus money and obtain access to other financial products and services provided by banks and non-bank financial institutions, and only if this potential demand is matched by financial intermediaries. Therefore, apart from examining the effect of remittances on financial deepening, this study empirically analyzes the effect of remittances on financial inclusion. For the analysis, we use panel data from 154 countries between 2004 and 2014 and explore whether and to what extent remittance inflows contribute to facilitating financial inclusion in these developing countries.[2]

The rest of this chapter is organized as follows. Section 5.2 reviews the relevant literature. Section 5.3 explains the definitions and sources of the data. Section 5.4 presents the model and explains the empirical technique. Section 5.5 shows the empirical results. Finally, Section 5.6 summarizes our main findings.

5.2　Literature Review

There are only a limited number of empirical analyses about the determinants of financial inclusion in general and financial access in particular. Relevant prior research particularly addressing remittances as the primary independent variable is more limited, consisting of Toxopeus and Lensink (2007), Ambrosius (2011), Demirgüç-Kunt *et al.* (2011), Aga and Martínez Pería (2014), and Anzoategui *et al.* (2014).

Toxopeus and Lensink (2007) investigate the effect of remittance inflows on financial inclusion using cross-country data on 64 developing countries. Financial inclusion is measured by the share of households with bank accounts. By estimating models in which

---

[2]Inoue and Hamori (2016) analyze the relationship between financial access and remittances using panel data from 38 developing countries in Asia and Oceania between 2001 and 2012. This chapter retains this analytical framework using panel data from 154 countries between 2004 and 2014. Furthermore, while Inoue and Hamori (2016) use two measures of financial access, that is, the logarithm of the number of commercial bank branches per 100,000 adults and the logarithm of the number of commercial bank branches per $1,000\,km^2$, this chapter uses the number of commercial bank branches per $1,000\,km^2$ as the measure of financial inclusion.

financial inclusion is explained by remittances per capita, the growth rate of GDP per capita, and other control variables, they find that an increase in remittances has a significantly positive effect on greater financial inclusion. In addition, by estimating a set of equations in which the growth rate of GDP per capita and financial inclusion are the endogenous variables, Toxopeus and Lensink (2007) confirm the hypothesis that remittances have a development effect through influences on financial inclusion.

Ambrosius (2011) analyzes how a change in remittance status affects financial access using Mexican household survey data for 2002 and 2005. Financial access is measured as two alternative dummy variables, each of which takes a value of 1 for households that improved their access status in terms of savings accounts or borrowing options. The results from the treatment effect model indicate that a change in remittance status has a statistically significant positive effect on both the ownership of savings accounts and the availability of borrowing options. Ambrosius (2011) demonstrates that these results are significant for rural households but not for urban households and that they are more important for microfinance institutions than for commercial banks.

Demirgüç-Kunt *et al.* (2011) analyze the effect of remittances on banking outreach, as well as banking depth, using municipal data for Mexico in 2000. The authors measure banking outreach by either the number of branches per capita or deposit accounts per capita, while they measure banking depth by the ratio of the amount of deposits to GDP and loans to GDP. Remittances refer to the percentage of households in each municipality that receive remittances. From a Tobit estimation, the authors find that remittances are significantly associated with greater banking outreach, that is, with an increasing number of branches and accounts per capita.[3]

Aga and Martínez Pería (2014) investigate the link between remittances and financial inclusion in five African countries, Burkina

---

[3]In addition, Demirgüç-Kunt *et al.* (2011) find a positive effect of remittances on bank deposits and loans, although the effect on bank loans is much smaller and much less robust.

Faso, Kenya, Nigeria, Senegal, and Uganda, using the World Bank's survey data, including about 10,000 households. Financial inclusion is measured by two alternative dummy variables, which take a value of 1 if any member of the household has a bank account or if the household opened a bank account after the migrant left the household, and 0 otherwise. Remittances are measured either by a dummy variable indicating if the household received remittances from a migrant residing abroad or by the amount of remittances received by the household in the past year prior to the survey year. The authors find that remittances increase the probability that the household opens a bank account in the five countries.

Finally, Anzoategui *et al.* (2014) explore the effect of remittances on financial inclusion in El Salvador using household survey data covering four periods between 1995 and 2001. The authors measure financial inclusion using three alternative dummy variables, which indicate whether households have a deposit account, apply for loans, or receive loans from formal financial institutions. Remittances refer to either a dummy variable indicating whether the household received remittances or the real amount of remittances per household member. The estimation results of the Probit regressions show that recipient households are more likely to have deposit accounts at formal financial institutions, while they are not more prone to request or receive loans from financial institutions.

Although the present study is closely related to the above-mentioned literature, it differs in the following respects. First, this study measures financial inclusion by the number of commercial bank branches per 1,000 km^2. Among the relevant literature, Demirgüç-Kunt *et al.* (2011) use either the number of branches per capita or deposit accounts per capita as the measure of banking outreach. Unlike Demirgüç-Kunt *et al.* (2011), we measure financial inclusion in terms of the geographical outreach of banking services.

The second difference is that instead of focusing on a specific country, we use the data for a large sample of countries. Among the studies in the literature, Toxopeus and Lensink (2007) use a cross-country dataset. Unlike them, we use panel data for 154 countries from 2004 to 2014, which has the advantage of incorporating a time dimension.

Through this study, we can examine whether the previous findings on a single country are applicable to a large sample of countries.

The third difference is that, in estimating the models, we apply the dynamic generalized method of moments (GMM) estimator to panel data. This allows us to deal with a potential endogeneity problem in the model.

5.3 Data

We use annual panel data from 2004 to 2014 for 154 countries. Table 5.1 provides the definition and data source of each variable. Financial inclusion (FI) is used as the dependent variable in this quantitative analysis. We measure the degree of financial inclusion by the number of commercial bank branches per 1,000 km^2. The data are derived from the Financial Access Survey of the International Monetary Fund (IMF) (2016). Figure 5.1 indicates the movement of average value of each year for FI. This figure shows that the degree of financial inclusion increases over time.

The most important explanatory variable in this study is REM, which represents personal remittances received and is defined as the percentage of GDP. The data for this variable are derived from

Table 5.1 Definition and Source of Each Variable

Variable	Definition	Source
FI	Number of commercial bank branches per 1,000 km^2	IMF (2016)
REM	Personal remittances, received, as a percentage of GDP	
GDP	Logarithm of real per capita GDP (constant 2005 US$)	
SCL	Gross primary school enrollment ratio, both sexes (%)	World Bank (2016)
$OPEN1$	Exports and imports of goods and services as a percentage of GDP	
$OPEN2$	Foreign direct investment net inflows, as a percentage of GDP	

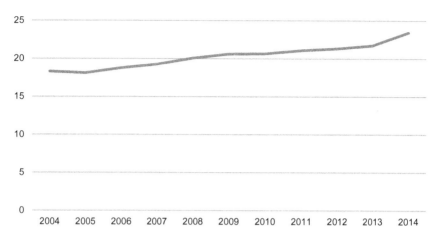

**Figure 5.1   Number of Commercial Bank Branches per 1,000 km²
(FI), Average Value of Each Year**

the World Development Indicators published by the World Bank
(2016). As Figure 5.2 illustrates, remittance inflows are assumed to
affect financial inclusion through several channels. For example, the
increase in remittance inflows enables recipient households to expand
their savings opportunities, which partly increases their demand
for deposit services at formal financial institutions. Furthermore,
remittances might allow recipient families to invest their surplus
funds, which partly increases the demand for financial products at
formal institutions. If this potential demand is matched by financial
intermediaries, an increase in migrants' remittances might contribute
to promoting financial inclusion in remittance-receiving countries.
Thus, the coefficient of REM in the model is expected to be positive.

As stated in Section 5.2, prior relevant studies are limited.
Therefore, with regard to the control variables, we refer to the closely
related literature that focuses on the financial deepening–remittances
nexus (e.g., Martínez Pería *et al.*, 2008; Gupta *et al.*, 2009; Aggarwal
et al., 2011; Chowdhury, 2011; Cooray, 2012; Brown *et al.*, 2013).
Among the regressors commonly used, we consider per capita GDP
(GDP), the primary school enrollment ratio (SCL), and economic
openness ($OPEN1$ and $OPEN2$) as control variables and take them
from the World Bank (2016).

Remittance Inflows

⇒ Consumption

⇒ Savings

→ Formal Channel → Demand for Deposit Bank Account

⇒ Financial Inclusion

→ Informal Channel → Savings under Mattresses

⇒ Investment

→ Formal Channel → Demand for Purchasing Financial

Products ⇒ Financial Inclusion

→ Informal Channel → Lending to Families and Neighbors

Figure 5.2 Transmission Channels from Remittance Inflows to Financial Inclusion

GDP is the logarithm of per capita GDP in constant 2005 US\$ and represents the level of economic development. A higher income level is likely to increase the demand for more formal financial services, such as deposits and remittances. Therefore, the coefficient of *GDP* in the model is expected to be positive.

SCL is the gross enrollment ratio for primary school and includes both sexes. When the school enrollment ratio increases, people might be more interested in the use of a financial mechanism as a tool to increase consumption and investment. Thus, the coefficient of *SCL* is expected to have a positive sign in the model.

*OPEN*1 indicates the sum of exports and imports as a percentage of GDP. We employ this variable as the measure of trade openness. *OPEN*2 represents net foreign direct investment (FDI) inflows as a percentage of GDP. This variable indicates the financial openness of the country. Trade and financial openness are expected to increase payments for exports, imports, and investment, which prompt exporters, importers, local firms, and foreign firms to access formal finance. Therefore, the coefficients of *OPEN*1 and *OPEN*2 in the model might be positive.

5.4   Model and Empirical Technique

We use a dynamic model to analyze the relationship between financial inclusion and remittances as follows:

$$FI_{i,t} = \beta_0 + \beta_1 FI_{i,t-1} + \beta_2 REM_{i,t} + \beta_3 REM_{i,t-1} + \beta_4 GDP_{i,t}$$

$$+\beta_5 SCL_{i,t} + \beta_6 OPEN1_{i,t} + \beta_7 OPEN2_{i,t} + u_{i,t}, \qquad (5.1)$$

where i denotes country and t denotes time; $FI_{i,t}$ denotes the measure of financial inclusion; $REM_{i,t}$ denotes remittances; $GDP_{i,t}$ denotes per capita GDP; $SCL_{i,t}$ denotes the primary school enrollment ratio; $OPEN1_{i,t}$ denotes the sum of exports and imports as a percentage of GDP; $OPEN2_{i,t}$ denotes FDI as a percentage of GDP; and $u_{i,t}$ is the error term.

When we analyze the relationship between financial inclusion and remittances, there is concern about an endogeneity problem. Anzoategui *et al.* (2014) point out that there are at least two reasons to deal with the endogeneity problem, which are as follows:

First, financial inclusion might reduce the costs of sending and receiving remittances and, hence, might make migrants more prone to send and households to receive remittances. Second, financial inclusion could finance migration, and, consequently, increase the remittance flow toward households with access to credit (Anzoategui *et al.*, 2014, p. 341).

To address this problem, we use a dynamic model expressed by Equation (5.1). In estimating the equation, we use the dynamic panel GMM estimator developed by Arellano and Bond (1991). This method takes the first differences of the model to eliminate fixed effects and then applies GMM to the first-difference model using valid instruments. The GMM estimator optimally exploits all the linear moment restrictions that follow from the assumption of no serial correlation in the error and uses the level of lagged variables as the instruments for the first-difference explanatory variables (Arellano and Bond, 1991). In this study, financial inclusion is used as the dynamic instrumental variable, and remittances, real per capita GDP, school enrolment ratio, and economic openness are used as the standard instrumental variables.

5.5 Empirical Results

Table 5.2 presents the empirical results of the dynamic panel model. Cases 1 and 2 report the results excluding and including the one-lagged value of remittances as the explanatory variable, respectively. In both cases, we use the number of commercial bank branches per $1,000\,\text{km}^2$ (FI) as a measure of financial inclusion. The results of the over-identifying restriction tests developed by Hansen (1982) are shown in this table as the J-statistic and its corresponding p-value. According to these results, the model specification is empirically supported for both cases.

Table 5.2 Empirical Results

	Case 1	Case 2
$FI\,(-1)$	0.900	0.897
	$(0.019)^{***}$	$(0.023)^{***}$
REM	0.570	1.741
	$(0.227)^{**}$	$(0.233)^{***}$
$REM\,(-1)$		-0.258
		$(0.058)^{***}$
GDP	2.767	3.651
	$(0.977)^{***}$	$(1.596)^{**}$
SCL	0.038	0.118
	(0.023)	$(0.037)^{***}$
$OPEN1$	0.029	0.044
	$(0.005)^{***}$	$(0.014)^{***}$
$OPEN2$	0.005	-0.002
	(0.007)	(0.007)
Number of cross-sections	140	140
Number of observations	858	858
J-statistic	38.327	42.853
p-value (J-statistic)	0.409	0.201

Notes: Robust t-statistics are shown in parentheses. ***, **, and * denote significance at the 1%, 5%, and 10% levels, respectively. Instrumental variables are chosen as follows. For both cases, dynamic panel instruments are $FI_{i,t-j}$, $(j = 2, \ldots)$; other instruments are $\Delta REM_{i,t-1}$, $\Delta GDP_{i,t-1}$, $\Delta SCL_{i,t-1}$, $\Delta OPEN1_{i,t-1}$, and $\Delta OPEN2_{i,t-1}$ (Δ denotes the first-difference values).

As is clear from Table 5.2, the coefficients of remittances (REM) are positive as expected and statistically significant in both cases (0.570 for Case 1 and 1.741 for Case 2). The coefficients of the one-lagged value of remittances are negative and statistically significant in Case 2, although the sum of these coefficients is positive (1.741 − 0.258 = 1.483 for Case 2). Thus, an increase in remittances has a significant and favorable effect on financial inclusion. Martínez Pería *et al.* (2008), Gupta *et al.* (2009), Aggarwal *et al.* (2011), Chowdhury (2011), Demirgüç-Kunt *et al.* (2011), and Cooray (2012) indicate that remittances have a positive effect on financial deepening. Unlike the findings of these works, our results show that remittances affect the promotion of financial inclusion.[4]

Regarding the control variables, Table 5.2 indicates that the coefficients of real per capita GDP (GDP) are estimated to be positive as expected and statistically significant at the 5% or 1% level in both cases (2.767 for Case 1 and 3.651 for Case 2). Thus, an increase in real per capita GDP has a positive effect on financial inclusion.

Next, the coefficients of the primary school enrollment ratio (SCL) are estimated to be positive (0.038 for Case 1 and 0.118 for Case 2) but statistically significant at the 1% level only in Case 2. Thus, a rise in the primary school enrollment ratio may positively affect financial inclusion.

In addition, the coefficients of trade openness ($OPEN1$) are estimated to be positive as expected and statistically significant at the 1% level in Cases 1 and 2. Thus, a rise in the degree of trade openness is likely to increase financial inclusion.

Finally, the coefficients of financial openness ($OPEN2$) are mixed, that is, positive for Case 1 and negative for Case 2. They are both statistically insignificant. Thus, the effect of financial openness on financial inclusion is not clear from the results obtained from our analysis.

---

[4]We also measure the degree of financial deepening by either outstanding loans from commercial banks as a percentage of GDP or outstanding deposits in commercial banks as a percentage of GDP and find that remittances have a statistically significant positive effect on financial deepening.

5.6   Concluding Remarks

Heretofore, empirical studies have found that financial deepening through formal and semi-formal financial intermediaries contributes to promoting economic growth and reducing poverty and income inequality. In addition, a growing body of empirical research has investigated the factors affecting the promotion of financial deepening. One of the potential leading factors is migrants' remittances. Indeed, most recent studies find that remittances are positively associated with financial deepening.

Unlike these previous studies, the present study focused on financial inclusion in terms of access to formal financial services and empirically analyzed whether and how remittances affect financial inclusion. Remittances are expected to contribute to promoting financial inclusion if unbanked recipient households become willing to demand the safe storage of surplus money and obtain access to other financial products and services provided by banks and non-bank financial institutions, and if these potential demands are matched by financial intermediaries.

In our empirical analysis, we considered models in which the number of commercial bank branches is explained by remittance inflows and control variables, including income level, school enrollment ratio, and economic openness. In estimating the models, we used unbalanced panel data from 154 countries between 2004 and 2014 to estimate the effect of remittances on financial inclusion. The empirical results indicate mainly that remittance inflows help to enlarge bank branch networks.

Migration is among the options for lower-income households with few employment opportunities within their country. If migrant transfers are available, hitherto unbanked recipient households are expected to demand formal financial products and services. By responding to this potential demand, formal financial institutions can achieve not only their public goal but also financial sustainability. Our empirical results show that remittances would become a catalyst for access to formal finance when potential customers come to understand the importance of formal finance and when financial service providers meet customer needs.

Regarding the control variables, we found from the dynamic GMM estimation that income level, school enrollment ratio, and trade openness have positive effects on financial inclusion. The results imply that higher income, higher school enrollment ratio, and greater trade openness are useful in promoting the access of hitherto unbanked customers to bank branches.

References

Aga, G. A., Martínez Pería, M. S., 2014. International remittances and financial inclusion in sub-Saharan Africa. World Bank Policy Research Working Paper 6991, World Bank, Washington D.C.

Aggarwal, R., Demirgüç-Kunt, A., Martínez Pería, M. S., 2011. Do remittances promote financial development? *Journal of Development Economics* 96, 255–264.

Ambrosius, C., 2011. Are remittances a 'catalyst' for financial access? Evidence from Mexico. *Proceedings of the German Development Economics Conference* 5.

Anzoategui, D., Demirgüç-Kunt, A., Martínez Pería, M. S., 2014. Remittances and financial inclusion: Evidence from El Salvador. *World Development* 54, 338–349.

Arellano, M., Bond, S., 1991. Some tests of specification for panel data: Monte Carlo evidence and an application to employment equations. *The Review of Economic Studies* 58, 277–297.

Brown, R. P. C., Carmignani, F., Fayad, G., 2013. Migrants' remittances and financial development: Macro- and micro-level evidence of a perverse relationship. *The World Economy* 36, 636–660.

Chowdhury, M. B., 2011. Remittances flow and financial development in Bangladesh. *Economic Modelling* 28, 2600–2608.

Cooray, A., 2012. Migrant remittances, financial sector development and the government ownership of banks: Evidence from a group of non-OECD economies. *Journal of International Financial Markets, Institutions and Money* 22, 936–957.

Demirgüç-Kunt, A., Córdova, E. L., Martínez Pería, M. S., Woodruff, C., 2011. Remittances and banking sector breadth and depth. *Journal of Development Economics* 95, 229–241.

Gupta, S., Pattillo, C. A., Wagh, S., 2009. Effect of remittances on poverty and financial development in sub-Saharan Africa. *World Development* 37, 104–115.

Hansen, L. P., 1982. Large sample properties of generalized method of moments estimators. *Econometrica* 50, 1029–1054.

Inoue, T., Hamori, S., 2016. Do workers' remittances promote access to finance? Evidence from Asia–Pacific developing countries. *Emerging Markets Finance and Trade* 52, 765–774.

International Monetary Fund (IMF), 2016. *Financial Access Survey.* IMF, Washington D.C., http://fas.imf.org/, Accessed 23 January 2016.

Martínez Pería, M. S., Mascaró, Y., Moizeszowicz, F., 2008. Do remittances affect recipient countries' financial development? in: Fajnzylber, P., López, J. H. (Eds.), *Remittances and Development: Lessons from Latin America.* World Bank, Washington D.C., pp. 171–215.

Toxopeus, H. S., Lensink, R., 2007. Remittances and financial inclusion in development. UNU-WIDER Research Paper 2007/49, United Nations University World Institute for Development, Helsinki.

World Bank, 2016. *World Development Indicators.* World Bank, Washington D.C., http://databank.worldbank.org/data/source/world-development-indicators, Accessed 23 January 2016.

Chapter 6

Financial Inclusion, Remittance Inflows, and Poverty Reduction: Complements or Substitutes?

6.1 Introduction

Conceptually, microfinance and international remittances are expected to reduce poverty by eliminating credit constraints on poor people and providing them with an additional income for consumption, investment, and savings. On the other hand, these sources of finance have different characteristics. For example, microfinance in general and microcredit in particular, in the form of borrowing from microfinance institutions (MFIs) with repayment obligations, are largely assumed to be used for productive investments to support local income-generating activities rather than for consumption. Furthermore, remittances are private incomes, which migrant workers send to their family members for household expenses without any restrictions on use. Thus, microfinance and remittances can serve as alternative sources of funds for the alleviation of poverty of their recipients.

Households in developing countries that require microfinance or migration and remittances are likely to belong to the same income class. Several micro-level analyses indicate that microcredit borrowing and migration can be interrelated processes. For example, based on a qualitative study of northwest Cambodia, Bylander

(2014) indicates that microcredit borrowing often works in tandem with migration and remittances and that microfinance is widely understood as a means of improving livelihoods by supplementing remittances in this rural area (*ibid.*, p. 293).

Several studies have analyzed the effect of either financial deepening or remittance inflows on poverty reduction in developing countries. By contrast, this chapter empirically examines whether financial inclusion through MFIs and remittances interact with each other in the process of poverty reduction at the macro level, and if so, to what extent.

Specifically, we estimate models in which the poverty headcount ratio is explained by financial inclusion, remittances, and their interaction term, as well as several other control variables, using a multi-country panel dataset. Because a lower poverty ratio indicates poverty reduction, a negative sign of the coefficients of financial inclusion, remittances, and their interaction term implies that financial inclusion and remittances have a synergistic effect on poverty reduction in developing countries. However, if financial inclusion and remittances have negative coefficients but the coefficient of the interaction term is positive, remittances have a greater poverty-alleviating effect in countries with a less inclusive financial system, and vice versa. These types of interactions have different policy implications for developing countries in their pursuit of poverty reduction strategies.

The rest of this chapter is structured as follows. Section 6.2 reviews the relevant literature. Section 6.3 presents the model and provides the definitions, sources, and properties of the data. Section 6.4 provides the empirical results. Section 6.5 summarizes our main findings.

6.2   Literature Review

With the growth of microfinance, an increasing number of empirical studies have analyzed the effect of microfinance on poverty in developing countries. Many of these studies investigate this issue using micro data on specific villages. Due to differences in the selected villages, types and amounts of data collected, and empirical techniques, the evidence from these studies is mixed.[1] However, a few recent empirical studies analyze this issue from a macro perspective using cross-country data.[2]

In Chapter 2 of this book, we examined the effect of financial inclusion through MFIs on the poverty headcount ratio using unbalanced panel data for 76 developing countries from 1995 to 2008. We measure the degree of financial inclusion alternatively by the number of MFIs per capita and the number of active borrowers per capita. In our model, the headcount ratio is explained by each indicator of financial inclusion and the control variables. From the generalized method of moments (GMM) estimation, we find that financial inclusion through microfinance contributes to alleviating poverty across developing countries.

Recently, Miled and Rejeb (2015) analyze the poverty-reducing effect of microcredit using cross-sectional data of 40 developing countries for 2011 as well as two-period (2000–2005 and 2006–2011) panel data of 57 developing countries. In their study, the dependent variable is either the poverty headcount ratio or household final consumption expenditure, while the main explanatory variable is MFIs' gross loan portfolio per capita. Their main result from the ordinary least squares and instrumental variable estimations is that MFIs' gross loan portfolio has a significantly negative relationship with the poverty ratio and a significantly positive relationship with household final consumption expenditure, confirming the role of microfinance in poverty reduction.

---

[1]Pitt and Khandker (1998), Mosley (2001), and Khandker (2005) conclude that microfinance loans increase the income and/or consumption of poor borrowers, whereas Coleman (1999), Morduch (1999), and Roodman and Morduch (2009) do not find similar results.

[2]Kai and Hamori (2009) and Hermes (2014) examine the effect of microfinance on income distribution using cross-sectional data on developing countries. Kai and Hamori (2009) measure the degree of microfinance intensity by the number of MFIs and the number of borrowers of MFIs, while Hermes (2014) measures it by the number of active borrowers relative to total population and total value of microfinance loans relative to GDP. They both find that microfinance intensity is negatively and significantly associated with income inequality, suggesting that in countries where microfinance intensity is higher, income inequality is lower.

In addition, Donou-Adonsou and Sylwester (2016) examine whether, and to what extent, banks and MFIs contribute to poverty reduction in developing countries. They apply the fixed-effects two-stage least squares estimation to a panel of 71 countries over the period 2002–2011 and estimate the models in which poverty is explained by financial deepening, per capita GDP, and the Gini index. Poverty is measured by the headcount ratio, poverty gap, or squared poverty gap, whereas financial deepening is measured by the ratio of bank credit to GDP or the ratio of MFI credit to GDP. Their results indicate that bank credit reduces poverty when poverty is measured by the headcount ratio or the poverty gap, but that MFI credit does not have any effect on poverty regardless of the measure employed.

At the same time, against the background of a surge in remittance inflows to developing countries, a growing body of literature has empirically analyzed the effect of this form of capital inflow on poverty reduction in developing countries, including the following studies: Adams and Page (2005), the International Monetary Fund (IMF) (2005), Jongwanich (2007), Gupta *et al.* (2009), Vargas-Silva *et al.* (2009), Anyanwu and Erhijakpor (2010), Serino and Kim (2011), the United Nations (2011), Imai *et al.* (2014), Gaaliche and Zayati (2015), and Azam *et al.* (2016). These studies empirically investigate the direct effect of remittances on poverty across countries using the poverty ratio, poverty gap, and squared poverty gap as poverty measures.

The findings of these studies differ slightly in some ways. For example, Adams and Page (2005) and Anyanwu and Erhijakpor (2010) indicate that remittance inflows have a statistically significant negative relationship with the poverty ratio, poverty gap, and squared poverty gap. On the other hand, Gupta *et al.* (2009) and Vargas-Silva *et al.* (2009) report that the poverty-reducing effect of remittances is not statistically significant when the squared poverty gap and the poverty ratio are used as measures of poverty, respectively.

Moreover, Adams and Page (2005), Jongwanich (2007), and Anyanwu and Erhijakpor (2010) indicate that the poverty-reducing effect is large, whereas the IMF (2005), Imai *et al.* (2014), and

Gaaliche and Zayati (2015) suggest that this effect is moderate. The United Nations (2011, p. 20) indicates that "remittances have stronger impact on poverty reduction if they are above the threshold of 5% of GDP of the country." Serino and Kim (2011) state that the poverty-reducing effect is uneven across poverty quintiles and that it tends to be more pronounced in the worst-off poverty group. Conversely, Azam *et al.* (2016) find that the positive effect of remittances on poverty alleviation is statistically significant only in upper middle-income countries. Despite these differences, relevant empirical studies conclude that remittance inflows generally alleviate poverty in developing countries.

6.3   Model and Data

Unlike the relevant literature, this chapter explores the effects of financial inclusion through MFIs and remittances on poverty simultaneously and examines whether, and to what extent, they interact with each other to alleviate poverty in developing countries. The dynamic model in this study is specified as follows:

$$POV_{i,t} = \alpha_0 + \alpha_1 POV_{i,t-1} + \alpha_2 FI_{i,t} + \alpha_3 REM_{i,t}$$
$$+ \alpha_4 FI_{i,t} \times REM_{i,t} + \alpha_5 X_{i,t} + u_{i,t}, \qquad (6.1)$$

where $POV_{i,t}$ is the poverty headcount ratio, $FI_{i,t}$ is financial inclusion, $REM_{i,t}$ is remittance inflows, $FI_{i,t} \times REM_{i,t}$ is the interaction term of financial inclusion and remittances, $X_{i,t}$ is the vector of control variables, and $u_{i,t}$ is the error term in country i at time t, with $i(= 1, 2, \ldots, N)$ being the number of cross-sections and $t(= 1, 2, \ldots, T)$ being the number of periods.

In the above equation, the poverty headcount ratio (POV) is used as the dependent variable. It is the percentage of the population in a country living on less than US\$ 1.25 per day at 2005 purchasing power parity prices. The data are obtained from the World Development Indicators of the World Bank (2014). A higher poverty ratio means a more impoverished condition.

The most important independent variable in our study is financial inclusion (FI). Financial inclusion represents the logarithm of the number of MFIs divided by the country's total population. The data for the number of MFIs are obtained from the Microfinance Information Exchange (MIX) (2010), while the population data are obtained from the World Bank (2014). Improving access to microfinance is believed to contribute to poverty reduction by eliminating credit constraints on poor people and increasing their productive assets and productivity. Accordingly, the coefficient of FI in Equation (6.1) is expected to be negative.

Remittances (REM) are the logarithm of the amount of personal remittances received divided by GDP. The data for REM are obtained from the World Bank (2014). An increase in migrants' remittances is also assumed to help lift their families out of poverty in the home countries by providing additional income for consumption, investment, and savings. Accordingly, the coefficient of REM in Equation (6.1) is expected to be negative.

The interaction term ($FI \times REM$) indicates the combined effect of financial inclusion and remittances in the poverty-alleviating process. The marginal effect of a change in remittances on poverty indicates the degree to which financial inclusion influences the effect of remittances on poverty. Given that financial inclusion and remittances have a poverty-reducing effect, a negative interaction term suggests that remittances can be regarded as a complement to financial inclusion. In this case, remittances and financial inclusion support each other and have a synergistic effect on poverty reduction in developing countries. However, if the coefficient of the interaction term has a positive sign, remittances can be regarded as a substitute for financial inclusion in the poverty-alleviating process. In this case, the poverty-reducing effect of remittances becomes larger in developing countries with a less inclusive financial system, and vice versa. We examine the signs and the significance of the interaction term.

Regarding the control variables, we apply the regressors frequently used in the literature as factors that influence poverty and take them from the World Bank (2014). One of the most powerful regressors among them is income growth. We consider the logarithm of real per capita GDP (GDP) to capture the average income of a sample country. Previous studies indicate that a higher level of income ameliorates the well-being of poor people (Ravallion and Chen, 1997; Ravallion, 2001; Dollar and Kraay, 2002; Besley and Burgess, 2003; Jalilian and Kirkpatrick, 2005). Therefore, the coefficient of GDP in Equation (6.1) is expected to be negative.

Several studies report that poor people's income rises nearly one-for-one with the average income. As such, economic policies and institutions have little effect on the share of poor people's income after accounting for the effect of average income (Roemer and Gugerty, 1997; Dollar and Kraay, 2002). Nonetheless, to confirm this finding, we add the other factors influencing poverty as control variables. These are the inflation rate, income inequality, and economic openness.

Inflation (INF) is defined by the annual change in consumer prices. Large and unpredictable price changes are considered to have a disproportionately negative effect on poor people because they are likely to have a larger share of cash in small portfolios and relatively limited instruments for hedging against inflation (Easterly and Fischer, 2001; Holden and Prokopenko, 2001). In line with previous studies, we expect the coefficient of INF to have a positive sign in Equation (6.1).

Income inequality, measured by the Gini index $(GINI)$, is considered to have a negative effect on poverty reduction (Ravallion, 2001; Besley and Burgess, 2003; Ravallion, 2005). If national income is kept constant, an increase in the Gini index implies a higher share of income for rich people and a lower share of income for poor people, or both. The latter two indicate the worsening of poverty. In addition, several studies state that a given rate of economic growth reduces poverty more in countries with low income inequality than in those with high income inequality (Ravallion, 1997; Adams and Page, 2005). Therefore, the coefficient of $GINI$ in Equation (6.1) is expected to be positive.

Economic openness $(OPEN)$ is measured by the sum of a country's exports and imports as a share of its GDP. Many theoretical and empirical studies have analyzed how economic openness affects poor people, especially those in developing countries. For example, Dollar and Kraay (2004) observe that in a large sample of countries, economic openness, measured in terms of trade integration, alleviates poverty. However, Hamori and Hashiguchi (2012) suggest that, in poor countries, globalization benefits only those with basic and high education and lowers the income share of those with no education. Because empirical studies have provided inconclusive evidence, we cannot *a priori* predict the sign of the coefficient of economic openness in the equation.

For the empirical analysis, we use unbalanced panel data for the period 1995–2013 for 119 countries. The data on financial inclusion are available until 2010. The sample consists of low-income, lower middle-income, and upper middle-income developing countries. The total number of observations lies between 163 and 180. Table 6.1 provides the definitions and sources of the data, while Table 6.2 presents summary statistics.

Table 6.1   Definition and Source of Each Variable

Variable	Definition	Source
POV	Poverty headcount ratio at US$ 1.25 a day as a percentage of the population	World Bank (2014)
FI	Logarithm of the number of microfinance institutions divided by the population	MIX (2010) (the population data from World Bank (2014))
REM	Logarithm of personal remittances, received, divided by GDP	World Bank (2014)
GDP	Logarithm of real per capita GDP (constant 2005 US$)	
INF	Inflation, consumer prices (%)	
GINI	GINI index (World Bank estimate) (%)	
OPEN	Exports and imports of goods and services as a percentage of GDP	

Table 6.2 Summary Statistics

Variable	Mean	Standard Deviation	Maximum	Minimum
POV	16.179	20.029	87.720	0.000
FI	−14.930	1.510	−11.902	−20.977
REM	−4.115	1.803	−0.478	−15.057
GDP	7.214	1.086	9.563	3.912
INF	16.380	116.281	4,145.110	−18.109
$GINI$	42.307	9.819	69.170	16.230
$OPEN$	81.458	37.805	223.597	14.772

6.4 Empirical Results

To estimate the panel data, we use the first-difference GMM. Because the explanatory variables include the lagged value of the explained variable, we cannot apply ordinary regression techniques. Furthermore, we need to address the potential endogeneity of explanatory variables. Accordingly, we estimate the model using the dynamic panel GMM estimators developed by Arellano and Bond (1991) to address the endogeneity problem.[3]

Table 6.3 presents the empirical results of the GMM estimation for the model expressed by Equation (6.1). In this table, the estimation results are divided into nine cases. In Cases 1 and 2, we use financial inclusion and remittances as the independent variables, respectively. In Case 3, we use both financial inclusion and remittances in estimating the equation, and in Case 4, we add the interaction term of financial inclusion and remittances. In Cases 5 to 8, we add the control variables (i.e., real per capita GDP, the inflation rate, the Gini index, and economic openness) individually. In Case 9, we include all the control variables together.

Table 6.3 reports the J-statistic and its associated p-value for each case. The J-statistic is used as a test for over-identifying moment conditions. As indicated by the table, the over-identifying

---

[3]For each model, the poverty ratio is used as the dynamic instrumental variable, and financial inclusion, remittances, and their interaction term are used as the standard instrumental variables.

Table 6.3 Empirical Results

	Case 1	Case 2	Case 3	Case 4	Case 5	Case 6	Case 7	Case 8	Case 9
POV(−1)	0.454	0.558	0.454	0.432	0.184	0.392	0.304	0.435	0.105
	(0.000)***	(0.000)***	(0.000)***	(0.001)***	(0.001)***	(0.002)***	(0.006)***	(0.000)***	(0.013)***
FI	−2.459		−2.391	−6.380	−4.128	−5.345	−5.492	−6.350	−2.234
	(0.000)***		(0.000)***	(0.086)***	(0.087)***	(0.033)***	(0.238)***	(0.025)***	(0.386)***
REM		−1.441	−0.529	−17.037	−13.386	−15.817	−19.149	−16.714	−9.476
		(0.000)***	(0.000)***	(0.399)***	(0.360)***	(0.161)***	(1.509)***	(0.136)***	(3.202)***
FI × REM				−1.200	−0.982	−1.033	−1.302	−1.205	−0.704
				(0.027)***	(0.026)***	(0.011)***	(0.095)***	(0.009)***	(0.164)***
GDP					−17.621				−14.142
					(0.087)***				(1.612)***
INF						0.077			0.092
						(0.000)***			(0.008)***
GINI							0.773		0.603
							(0.002)***		(0.025)***
OPEN								−0.033	−0.067
								(0.000)***	(0.021)***
J-statistic	550.267	19.040	27.818	316.552	28.456	0.414	27.736	28.881	22.143
p-value (J-statistic)	(0.000)	(0.939)	(0.474)	(0.000)	(0.440)	(1.000)	(0.371)	(0.418)	(0.391)
Number of observations	180	188	180	180	176	170	172	180	163

Notes: Standard errors are reported in parentheses. The dependent variable is the poverty headcount ratio (*POV*). *FI* denotes the logarithm of the number of MFIs per capita. *REM* denotes the logarithm of the ratio of personal remittances to GDP. *GDP* denotes the logarithm of real per capita GDP. *INF* denotes the growth rate of the consumer price index. *GINI* denotes the Gini index. *OPEN* denotes the sum of exports and imports per GDP.*** indicates statistical significance at the 1% level.

restriction cannot be rejected at the 5% level of significance in any case except Cases 1 and 4. Therefore, the model specification is generally supported empirically.

The main findings are as follows. The coefficients of financial inclusion (FI) are estimated to be negative, ranging from -6.380 to -2.234. They are statistically significant at the 1% level in all cases. The empirical results also indicate that the coefficients of remittances (REM) are negative, ranging from -19.149 to -0.529. They are statistically significant at the 1% level in all cases. Therefore, the coefficients of FI and REM are statistically significant and have the expected signs, suggesting that increasing the coverage of MFIs and remittance inflows significantly reduce poverty in developing countries. These results are consistent with the relevant literature mentioned in Section 6.2.

Furthermore, Table 6.3 indicates that the coefficients of the interaction term ($FI \times REM$) are negative, ranging from -1.302 to -0.704, and statistically significant at the 1% level in all cases. Considering the negative effects of financial inclusion and remittances on the poverty ratio, this result suggests that financial inclusion and remittances complement each other in the poverty-alleviating process. In other words, financial inclusion and remittances have a synergistic effect on poverty reduction in developing countries.

Regarding the control variables, Table 6.3 indicates that their coefficients are statistically significant with the expected signs. The coefficients of real per capita GDP (GDP) are estimated to be negative (-17.621 in Case 5 and -14.142 in Case 9) and statistically significant at the 1% level in both cases. Thus, an increase in per capita GDP has a positive effect on poverty reduction. The coefficients of inflation (INF) are estimated to be positive (0.077 in Case 6 and 0.092 in Case 9) and statistically significant at the 1% level in both cases. Thus, a rise in the inflation rate negatively affects poverty reduction. Regarding the effect of income inequality, the coefficients of the Gini index ($GINI$) are estimated to be positive (0.773 in Case 7 and 0.603 in Case 9) and statistically significant at the 1% level in both cases. Thus, a rise in the degree of income inequality worsens poverty in developing countries. Regarding the effect of economic openness on the poverty ratio, the coefficients of exports and imports as a share of GDP ($OPEN$) are estimated to be negative (-0.033 in Case 8 and -0.067 in Case 9) and statistically significant at the 1% level in both cases. Therefore, economic openness contributes to poverty reduction in developing countries.

In summary, it is clear from Table 6.3 that financial inclusion and remittance inflows improve the poverty ratio, while complementing each other in the poverty-alleviating process. These results hold even when the control variables are included. Regarding the control variables, increases in the income level and economic openness ameliorate the poverty ratio, whereas higher inflation and rising inequality exacerbate it.

6.5   Concluding Remarks

Recently, several empirical studies have analyzed the effects of financial inclusion and remittances on poverty reduction in developing countries from a macro perspective. The relevant literature generally indicates that the increasing breadth of the financial system and remittances help ameliorate poverty. Our study contributes to the literature by considering the combined effects of financial inclusion through MFIs and remittances on poverty reduction. This study empirically examines whether these financial factors interact with each other to alleviate poverty in developing countries, and if so, to what extent.

We estimated the models in which the poverty indicator is explained by financial inclusion, remittance inflows, and their interaction term, as well as other standard control variables applying the GMM to the panel data on 119 developing countries for the period 1995–2013. We found that the coefficients of financial inclusion and remittances have significant negative values, suggesting that financial inclusion and remittances help alleviate poverty in developing countries. These results are consistent with those of relevant previous studies.

In addition, we found negative and significant coefficients for the interaction term of financial inclusion and remittance inflows.

Given the poverty-reducing effects of financial inclusion and remittances, this result suggests that financial inclusion and remittances complement each other in the poverty-alleviating process. In other words, financial inclusion and remittances have a synergistic effect on poverty reduction in developing countries. Therefore, poor people in developing countries can further improve their standards of living by gaining greater access to MFIs, borrowing more funds from them, and receiving more remittances from their family members working abroad. The abovementioned results hold even after the control variables are included, both individually and together.

Microfinance and remittances are not distributed evenly across developing countries. Figure 6.1 depicts the combination of these financing sources in each sample country, normalized by the country's GDP. According to this, some developing countries have already had sufficient funds from both sources of finance. However, many

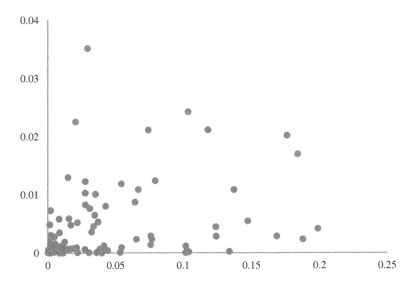

Figure 6.1   Combination of Microfinance and Remittances in Sample Countries

Notes: The vertical axis shows the gross loan portfolio of microfinance institutions as a share of GDP. The horizontal axis shows the amount of remittance inflows as a share of GDP.

Sources: MIX (2010) and World Bank (2014).

other countries have insufficient funds from either microfinance or remittances, or both. Therefore, based on our findings, we recommend that governments in developing countries, especially those with insufficient funds from microfinance and remittances, use either or both sources of finance to reduce poverty. To ensure that poor people can make use of microfinance and remittances to improve their living standards, policymakers in developing countries should work in cooperation with the international community to strengthen regulations on the lending behavior of MFIs and reduce transaction fees on migrants' remittances through formal channels.

Finally, regarding the control variables, we confirm that increase in the income level and economic openness ameliorates the poverty ratio, whereas higher inflation and rising inequality exacerbate it. These results for control variables are consistent with those of prior studies.

References

Adams Jr, R. H., Page, J., 2005. Do international migration and remittances reduce poverty in developing countries? *World Development* 33, 1645–1669.

Anyanwu, J. C., Erhijakpor, A. E. O., 2010. Do international remittances affect poverty in Africa? *African Development Review* 22, 51–91.

Arellano, M., Bond, S., 1991. Some tests of specification for panel data: Monte Carlo evidence and an application to employment equations. *The Review of Economic Studies* 58, 277–297.

Azam, M., Haseeb, M., Samsudin, S., 2016. The impact of foreign remittances on poverty alleviation: Global evidence. *Economics & Sociology* 9, 264–281.

Besley, T., Burgess, R., 2003. Halving global poverty. *Journal of Economic Perspectives* 17, 3–22.

Bylander, M., 2014. Borrowing across borders: Migration and microcredit in rural Cambodia. *Development and Change* 45, 284–307.

Coleman, B. E., 1999. The impact of group lending in Northeast Thailand. *Journal of Development Economics* 60, 105–141.

Dollar, D., Kraay, A., 2002. Growth is good for the poor. *Journal of Economic Growth* 7, 195–225.

Dollar, D., Kraay, A., 2004. Trade, growth, and poverty. *The Economic Journal* 114, F22–F49.

Donou-Adonsou, F., Sylwester, K., 2016. Financial development and poverty reduction in developing countries: New evidence from banks and microfinance institutions. *Review of Development Finance* 6, 82–90.

Easterly, W., Fischer, S., 2001. Inflation and the poor. *Journal of Money, Credit and Banking* 33, 160–178.

Gaaliche, M., Zayati, M., 2015. The causal relationship between remittances and poverty reduction in developing country: Using a non-stationary dynamic panel data. *Journal of Globalization Studies* 6, 30–39.

Gupta, S., Pattillo, C. A., Wagh, S., 2009. Effect of remittances on poverty and financial development in sub-Saharan Africa. *World Development* 37, 104–115.

Hamori, S., Hashiguchi, Y., 2012. The effect of financial deepening on inequality: Some international evidence. *Journal of Asian Economics* 23, 353–359.

Hermes, N., 2014. Does microfinance affect income inequality? *Applied Economics* 46, 1021–1034.

Holden, P., Prokopenko, V., 2001. Financial development and poverty alleviation: Issues and policy implications for developing and transition countries. IMF Working Paper WP/01/160, International Monetary Fund, Washington D.C.

Imai, K. S., Gaiha, R., Ali, A., Kaicker, N., 2014. Remittances, growth and poverty: New evidence from Asian countries. *Journal of Policy Modeling* 36, 524–538.

International Monetary Fund (IMF), 2005. *World Economic Outlook April 2005: Globalization and External Imbalances.* IMF, Washington D.C.

Jalilian, H., Kirkpatrick, C., 2005. Does financial development contribute to poverty reduction? *Journal of Development Studies* 41, 636–656.

Jongwanich, J., 2007. Workers' remittances, economic growth and poverty in developing Asia and the Pacific countries. UNESCAP Working Paper WP/07/01, United Nations Economic and Social Commission for Asia and the Pacific, Bangkok.

Kai, H., Hamori, S., 2009. Microfinance and inequality. *Research in Applied Economics* 1, 1–12.

Khandker, S. R., 2005. Microfinance and poverty: Evidence using panel data from Bangladesh. *The World Bank Economic Review* 19, 263–286.

Microfinance Information Exchange (MIX), 2010. *Indicators for Microfinance Institutions.* MIX, Washington D.C., http://www.mixmarket.org/mfi/indicators, Accessed 19 August 2010.

Miled, K. B. H., Rejeb, J.-E. B., 2015. Microfinance and poverty reduction: A review and synthesis of empirical evidence. *Procedia — Social and Behavioral Sciences* 195, 705–712.

Morduch, J., 1999. The microfinance promise. *Journal of Economic Literature* 37, 1569–1614.

Mosley, P., 2001. Microfinance and poverty in Bolivia. *Journal of Development Studies* 37, 101–132.

Pitt, M. M., Khandker, S. R., 1998. The impact of group-based credit programs on poor households in Bangladesh: Does the gender of participants matter? *Journal of Political Economy* 106, 958–996.

Ravallion, M., 1997. Can high-inequality developing countries escape absolute poverty? *Economic Letters* 56, 51–57.

Ravallion, M., 2001. Growth, inequality and poverty: Looking beyond averages. *World Development* 29, 1803–1815.

Ravallion, M., 2005. Inequality is bad for the poor. World Bank Policy Research Working Paper 3677, World Bank, Washington D.C.

Ravallion, M., Chen, S., 1997. What can new survey data tell us about recent changes in distribution and poverty? *The World Bank Economic Review* 11, 357–382.

Roemer, M., Gugerty, M. K., 1997. Does economic growth reduce poverty? CAER II Discussion Paper 4, Harvard Institute for International Development, Cambridge.

Roodman, D., Morduch, J., 2009. The impact of microcredit on the poor in Bangladesh: Revisiting the evidence. CGD Working Paper 174, Center for Global Development, Washington D.C.

Serino, M. N. V., Kim, D., 2011. How do international remittances affect poverty in developing countries? A quantile regression analysis. *Journal of Economic Development* 36, 17–40.

United Nations, 2011. *Impact of Remittances on Poverty in Developing Countries.* United Nations, New York and Geneva.

Vargas-Silva, C., Jha, S., Sugiyarto, G., 2009. Remittances in Asia: Implications for the fight against poverty and the pursuit of economic growth. ADB Economics Working Paper Series 182, Asian Development Bank, Manila.

World Bank, 2014. *World Development Indicators.* World Bank, Washington D.C., http://databank.worldbank.org/data/source/world-development-indicators, Accessed 5 November 2014.

Index